"The Christian Journey"
&
The Lay Ministry
Week-end

by :Donald C. Taft

authorHOUSE®

AuthorHouse™
1663 Liberty Drive, Suite 200
Bloomington, IN 47403
www.authorhouse.com
Phone: 1-800-839-8640

First published by AuthorHouse 4/7/2009

ISBN: 978-1-4389-3621-5 (sc)

Library of Congress Control Number: 2009900007

Printed in the United States of America
Bloomington, Indiana

This book is printed on acid-free paper.

I have been involved with church renewal since the mid –70's when I attended a Cel-LAY-bration of 1000 Lay Renewal Week-ends in Southern Baptist life in Atlanta Georgia. I was astonished that I had never heard of church renewal until that point. I might add, that even today, over 30 years later, I still run into Southern Baptists who have never heard of or experienced church renewal. This is a book for Christians and the journey they are engaged in. It is not intended primarily for the non-believer, but it might be useful, nevertheless, in the search for faith.

Following that introduction to renewal, almost every October, in the beautiful mountains of NW Georgia at the Georgia Baptist Assembly, my wife and I, along with hundreds of other lay leaders, together with pastors and others interested in church renewal, gathered to converse about what God seemed to be saying to the church. At those yearly conferences, I had the opportunity to personally meet and converse with many Christian leaders and authors of that day; men like Ralph Neighbor, James Mahoney, David Haney, Reid Harden, and of course, the man considered to be the 'father of church renewal', Dr. Findley Edge, all of whom profoundly either changed my view of what God wanted from the church or confirmed it. In addition, men like Dr. Emory Campbell, my pastor for a brief time in Southern California deeply influenced my life as have Ed Bullock, George Crouch, Bob Foy, David Langford, Ken Smith, John Truitt, who lived Romans 12: 1&2, and last, but certainly not least, Henry (Chick) Byrd, a close and insightful friend. The writings of Rick

Warren, John Ortberg, John Maxwell and Philip Yancey have also meant a great deal to me. So what follows is a tribute to these and to many others – spiritual heroes of mine. Their words are incorporated into my text as a living part of who I am.

The Church Renewal Journey has three main phases. The first step is the Lay Renewal Week-end. A team from other churches lead out in testimonies and facilitating small groups during the week-end. Of course there is singing and a lot of one on one conversations about the reality of the Christian faith during the week-end. Outside team members stay in the homes of church members where life-long friendships are established. The key statement during this first phase of the Journey is this : "God knows me and desires to use *me* in His work in the world." Small groups are formed after the week-end to continue the discussion of what it means to be a Christian.

After six months to a year later, the church may be ready for the second phase of the Journey called, The Lay Ministry Week-end. The format this time is roughly the same with the addition of an outside teacher and four teaching sessions centering on the SHAPE acronym created by Rick Warren to explain how God prepares His people for service in the world. The small groups this time focus on the statement : "God has gifted me and 'shaped' me for ministry in the world. "

There is a third week-end that follows again after a period of time. That week-end is called the Marketplace/ Evangelism Week-end where the teaching is aimed at motivating followers of Christ to take their faith with them into their marketplace. The key statement here is : "God desires to use me in my marketplace."

This book is the presentation I created for the second week-end in the Church Renewal process called "Discovering My S.H.A.P.E. for Ministry".

Donald C. Taft

Special Thanks and Dedicated To :

My sister Dr. Marilyn Thomas for her encouragement and tips for editing and publishing

My pastor, Rev. Bobby Morrow and Assoc. Sr. Pastor Stan Heiser for their encouragement

My Church Renewal colleagues, Bob Foy and Lionel Hahn whose creativity and enthusiasm for renewal never wavers

My sister-in-law, Jane Harris and Dr. Byrns Coleman, Professor of Religion at Wingate University for their extremely helpful editing and structure suggestions

My wife Anita without whom this book would never have been started or finished

Dozens of pastors and thousands of lay people in churches all over America who asked for this book to be made available and for whom Church Renewal has brought new joy in serving the Lord of their lives

Contents

CHAPTER I

In Dr. Edge's book, <u>The Greening of the Church</u>, which saw its first printing almost 40 years ago, Dr. Edge quotes Charlie Shedd with the following which is so frighteningly true even today : "The problem is not that the churches are filled with empty pews, but (rather) the pews are filled with empty people !" We seem to believe that our problem is empty pews – as in, "Come to my church, come hear my pastor." Dr. Edge seems to be saying to the church of his day and perhaps to our day as well, "Stop focusing so much attention on the empty pews and start focusing on the emptiness of the people sitting in those pews. "If the people who are coming to our services were truly filled with God's Holy Spirit and were thrilled with what they experienced on Sunday mornings, we wouldn't have a problem with empty pews." The point of course is that when God's people understand more of what God can do in their own lives, they want to and will share it with others with whom they come into contact.

Here's another quote from Dr. Edge's book : "A majority of our church members have no clear understanding of who they are or what they have been called to be or to do as the

'People of God' !" Despite the time we spend together in worship and Bible Study on Sundays and Wednesdays, we don't know to whom we belong or what we are supposed to be doing as Christians on a daily basis. We don't understand how our lives are supposed to be any different from the non-Christians who live alongside us, and go to work just like we do. No wonder survey after survey tells us that the lives of those **in the church** look no different than those **outside of the church**.

One final quote from Dr. Edge : "The average church member's understanding of what it means to be a Christian is so shallow and superficial as to constitute a major perversion of the Gospel !" He says basically that we are making up our own Gospel to fit our lifestyles rather than adopting our lifestyles to fit the real Gospel. I have often wondered what the responses would be if we took a survey right after our worship service as people were exiting the sanctuary and asked them the following questions, "What does it mean for you to be a Christian ?" "What are you supposed to be doing on a daily basis as a follower of Christ ?" "How is your life any different from another 'good person' who does good things for others daily ?" I suspect the answers would shock us : "I pay my taxes on time." "I don't cheat on my wife." "I treat my kids well and provide for them to the best of my ability," or, "In all honesty, I don't know!" Some of these answers may be commendable, but hardly what Dr. Edge would call the Christian lifestyle.

But what about today ? Are we in better shape today ? In a survey of 38,000 Americans, the Pew Forum on Religion recently reported the following :

90% of Americans believe in God. Well, that's a pretty good start, right ?

75% of Americans believe heaven is a place where people who have led good lives are eternally rewarded. What do you think about that one ? Is that what you believe ? Is that belief in the Bible ?

How about this one ?

70% of those affiliated with a religion believe that many religions, not just their own, can lead to eternal salvation. Is **that** in your Bible ?

And finally,

Only 25% believe there is only one true way to interpret their own religious teachings !

Here is another example of where we are today in the church : In Eddie Hammett's book <u>Reaching People Under 40 While Keeping People Over 60</u>, he says this :

Fewer than half of those who say they are affiliated with any Christian church in America attend on any given week. Or this :

In the decade from 1990 – 2001, those who identified themselves as secular and having no religion grew by 110% !

Or this :

At the present rate of change, most Americans will be non-Christian by the year 2035.

A modern church consultant and statistician states it this way : "Americans appear somewhat willing to **attend** church, read the Bible, and even make a small offering, but most stop short of establishing new priorities or making a tangible commitment to knowing or loving God." Well, that's certainly clear! In my experience, it appears to be true also! We Christians **do** seem to be willing to attend, at least infrequently, some **are** reading the Bible, some even make a regular offering, but the evidence of the establishment of any new priorities or the making of a life commitment to knowing or loving their God is not terribly obvious.

It seems that church today is so focused on getting people to **come**, that for the average lay person, **that** becomes the goal, attending. For many Christians, perhaps even the majority, their response to the invitation that God gives to them, through Christ, to take on the ministry of reconciliation (II Corinthians 5:17, 18) is to attend church on Sunday and perhaps on Wednesday as well. **Coming has become the goal for far too many Christians!** Tony Campolo says, "You Southern Baptists are so used to telling the world "Y'all come", come to my church, come hear my pastor, that you can't hear Jesus saying to you, **you all go!**" And I might add, if we were **going** into our world, into our marketplace with the Gospel of Christ, we wouldn't have trouble with people coming!

A national Christian leader once said it correctly : "We must move from simply gathering Christians to mobilizing them to scatter throughout their communities and world – Christians who are on mission for the Lord whom they serve."

What is going on here ? What is serving Christ all about ?

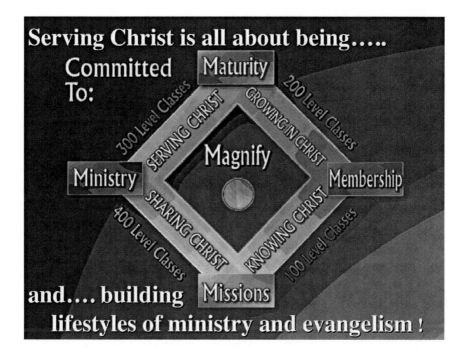

Serving Christ is all about being.....
Committed To: Maturity

300 Level Classes — SERVING CHRIST — GROWING IN CHRIST — 200 Level Classes

Ministry — Magnify — Membership

400 Level Classes — SHARING CHRIST — KNOWING CHRIST — 100 Level Classes

and.... building Missions
lifestyles of ministry and evangelism !

We are indebted to Rick Warren who created the baseball diamond analogy for describing what Christians **should** be all about as he illuminates what he calls the five purposes of the church – Membership, Maturity, Ministry, Missions and Magnify.

First base, or Membership, represents a decision by a person to **become** a Christian – beginning the process Warren describes as *knowing Christ*.

Then Second base, or Maturity, describes a Christian as he or she *grows in Christ*, adding the life disciplines of prayer, meditation of scripture, fellowship, and tithing.

Third base, or Ministry, represents a Christian *serving Christ* as he or she discovers the five ways God prepares His people for service (more on that momentarily).

Home plate, or Missions represents the Christian *living a lifestyle of sharing Christ*, the Good News, with others. In other words, after becoming a Christian and acquiring the habits necessary for a disciplined Christian life, the Christian embarks on a continuing quest of discovery, of how and where Christ would have him or her serve and share the Good News with others.

All of this then produces the last purpose of the church, Magnify or Worship. Warren's point is that Christians worship their God with their lives, not just on Sunday morning at a specific time or place. Therefore, Christians should be about the process of building lifestyles of ministry and evangelism. – i.e. **Being** Good News (Ministry) and **Telling** Good News (Evangelism). These two are flip sides of the same Christian Lifestyle coin – One side is Ministry and the other side is Evangelism. **This** is what Christians are supposed to be about then – building **lifestyles** of ministry and evangelism.

If this is what we are supposed to be about, then why are so many of us committed to so many other things ? The answer appears to be that as Christians, we don't know or we have forgotten who we are and what we are to be about ! So who are we then and what have we been called to be and to do ?

First of all, we are His – the Body of Christ – believers in God's Son and we know that all believers are called, gifted, equipped and sent. Let's take these one at a time.

All believers are **called**. Turn to II Corinthians 5: 17-18 and read what Paul tells the believers at Corinth about this subject.

> *"Therefore, if anyone is in Christ, he is a new creation; the old has gone and the new has come! All this is from God, who reconciled us to Himself through Christ and gave us (those of us who believe in Him) the ministry of reconciliation…"* NIV

As a believer in Christ then, I have the overall call, which I share with all Christians, to the ministry of reconciliation. God is calling me to partner with Him in His reconciling work in the world. Everything I do then as a Christian has reconciliation as its heart. All of my Christian service, all of my good deeds, everything points others to the God I serve. This is the core of what it means to be called to the ministry of reconciliation.

But, I am also **gifted – spiritually gifted**. In Romans 12: 6-8, Paul explains this to the believers in Rome.

> *"We have different gifts, according to the grace given us. If a man's gift is prophesying, let him use it in proportion to his faith. If it is serving, let him serve; if it is teaching, let him teach; if it is encouraging, let him encourage; if it is contributing to the needs of others, let him give generously; if it is leadership, let him govern diligently; if it is showing mercy, let him do it cheerfully." NIV*

We will have much more to say on the subject of Spiritual Gifts later. But, for now, it is sufficient to say that as Christians, **we are spiritually gifted by God's Holy Spirit so that we can carry out the ministry He has for us.**

I am also equipped for my ministry. I once heard a pastor say, "God doesn't always call the equipped, but He always equips those He calls." In Ephesians 4: 11-12, Paul reminds the believers at Ephesus :

> *"It was He who gave some to be apostles, some to be prophets, some to be evangelists, and some to be pastors and teachers to prepare God's people for works of service...." NIV*

Who are these people in your life ? These are the people you can name who have been responsible to a significant degree for your Christian growth. It is probably not a large number for most people. In many ways, these people can be viewed as gifts from God, helping to equip you for the service He has planned for you.

And finally, **He has sent you** into the world to meet the needs of those you encounter and always to point them to the

God you serve. In John 17:18; 20-23, we find these words of Jesus Himself :

> *"As you sent Me into the world, I have sent them into the world.* ***My prayer is not for them alone.*** *I pray also for those who will believe in Me through their message. That all of them may be one Father, just as You are in Me and I am in You. May they also be in Us so that the world may believe that You have sent Me. ... May they be brought to complete unity to let the world know that You sent Me and have loved them even as You have loved Me."* NIV

Jesus begins by praying for His disciples, but then the prayer abruptly changes and He changes the subject when He says, "My prayer is not for them alone." He says His prayer is also for those who will believe in Him through their words, i.e., the words of the disciples who were there. That prayer is for all believers – for me and for you ! Think about that – Jesus praying for me, He is sending me out into the world. Why ? So that we might be united in our effort to tell the world about Him and that God sent Him to us – Wow ! I can't get over it – Jesus praying specifically for me !

So there you have it. All believers are called, gifted, equipped and sent into the world, a world dying to know Him. In order to do that, as Christians, we must develop lifestyles of ministry and evangelism – being Good News and telling Good News. That's who we are and what we've been called to be and to do !

CHAPTER 2

Now, let's talk about this word – Ministry ! When we speak of a church's ministry, what exactly is it that makes up a church's ministry ? Any church's ministry is determined by two things : God's purposes and the make-up or SHAPE of its congregation. First of all, the church must be able to answer the question, "Why has God allowed this church to continue here, at this place, at this time ?" What is our purpose at this point in our history ? The church might be 100, 150 or even 200 years old, but what does God expect from us **now** ? And just what **is** God's purpose ? God's purpose is the same as it has always been – reconciliation - bringing all of His creation back into fellowship with Him. That's what God has always desired. When you think about it, the Bible is filled with stories of how God is constantly calling the people back into fellowship with Him.

What about your personal ministry – that special place which God has for you to minister to others ? How do you find that ? You start by looking closely at how God has SHAPED you. Your goal as a Christian is to **discover** the way God has SHAPED you, molded you, or prepared you for that ministry. The results of discovering this ministry you've been SHAPED for are two fold : First of all, you have a deep sense of fulfillment – at last, when it all comes together and you hear yourself saying, "**This** is the place God has for me". That brings a sense of life fulfillment which is hard to describe. Secondly, finding that special place of service also brings with it a strong sense of fruitfulness as you see God working through you, producing fruit in the lives of others.

Where does this word ministry come from anyway ? The word ministry comes from the Greek word "diakonos" meaning 'to execute for the common good of others' or simply, 'to serve'. This is also where we get the word Deacon and the suggestion that a Deacon's role is to serve. The best definition that I have found for Ministry is "Using whatever God has given you to serve Him and to meet the needs of others".

The best way I can suggest for finding your ministry is a 5 step process which is detailed below. I will not spend equal time on each segment. However, step one **is** crucially important and that will generate the most comments, for everything rides on your answer to one critical question, Are you willing to :

Step 1 : Dedicate Your Body

James Mahoney, author of <u>Journey Into Usefulness,</u> once described Romans 12: 1 & 2 to me personally as the two most important verses in all the New Testament for Christians who want to grow. Let's look at these two verses more closely. Paul tells the church at Rome:

*"I beseech you therefore, brethren, by the mercies of God, that **ye present your bodies a living sacrifice**, holy acceptable unto God, which is your*

*reasonable service. And be ye not conformed to this world; **but be ye transformed** by the renewing of your mind, that ye may prove what is that good, and acceptable, and perfect will of God   KJV*

Paul seems to be saying, "I urge you to make your bodies a living sacrifice. It would be reasonable (the Greek word is "logikin" or logical in English) for you to do this if you understood what Jesus did for you on the cross. He gave His life for you and now it is 'logical' for you to give your life back to Him or rather, to live for His purposes instead of your own.

He continues, "If you do this (Verse 2), you will no longer look like the world around you. You will acquire different goals, motivations, a new life purpose. In other words, you will be transformed, or changed from the inside out. Your motivation will now come from within, not from someone else outside of you. This is motivation that is hard for the world to understand. We are used to someone saying, "Come go with me to the homeless shelter this week-end and I won't call on you for six months." This new motivation, on the other hand, is produced from within and is 'God-driven'. These people will find a way to serve if you try to stop them. They simply can't not serve !

And finally, Paul ends with, "…that you may know and then see (prove) that God's will for you is good, acceptable and perfect". **You can know God's will for your life.** But…. it begins with making your life a life of sacrifice – deciding to live for God's purpose rather than for your own. I can almost hear Paul saying, "Why do you want to know what God's will is for your life unless you have decided to do it ? Perhaps you just want to compare God's will with your own and decide which one you **like** best ? Why do you want to know what your Spiritual Gift is unless you have decided to use it for His purpose ? Or is it just curiosity ?

After all, isn't this the way most of us learned how to deal with the world's tough decisions ? My dad taught me to list all the pros and cons of a decision and then to see which one looks best and then make the call saying, which way is best for me? But how do you decide whether or not to do God's will if you don't know what it is ? This is the problem with taking the world's concepts of living and applying them to spiritual growth. To me, Paul seems to be saying, first, we make the decision to follow God's will for our lives (Make your life a life of sacrifice – live for **His** purposes), without even knowing what that will is and then he reveals His will to us, not all at once, of course, but step by step, as we are ready to act.

A missionary friend of mine brought this into sharp focus for me one day. He asked me why the members of churches back home in America where he spoke regularly, were amazed at the **sacrifice** he and his wife were making by serving in foreign lands. "Where is the sacrifice ?", he asked. I responded that it must be what they saw as sacrifice would be living without some of the everyday conveniences we sometimes take for granted – like electrical power available every day, all day long - or telephone service that worked 100% of the time – or being able to purchase literally whatever we wanted (and could afford), 24/7 or - being able to spend time with loved ones for important dates like birthdays, holidays and/or anniversaries. He slowly indicated to me that he understood that, but then he made this comment, "It's just that to me, sacrifice means giving up what I want to do, to do what God wants me to do, and I'm not doing that. **I am doing what I want to do, so you see, for me, <u>there is no sacrifice</u>.**"

Then it hit me. What looks like sacrifice to me is not necessarily sacrifice to someone like my missionary friend. Perhaps Paul was not speaking about the kind of artificial sacrifice we speak of sometimes, like, "I'm sacrificing my Saturday; instead of playing golf, I'll be working at the homeless shelter." Paul wasn't talking about giving up what we want to do in order to do what God wanted us to do. He's talking about making a decision to follow Christ and to do the Father's will even perhaps before you know what it is and then, God will begin His transforming power within you (…but be ye transformed, or as I understand the Greek, you will be transformed), changing your 'wanter' so that after a time, what you want and what God wants are inseparable, i.e. I can't tell the difference any longer between the two. My missionary friend, you see, had made the decision to do God's will whatever it was and wherever it took him, what I call 'crossing the river'. When you cross the river, or decide to follow God's will perhaps without knowing what it is, you are forever changed and God reveals His plan to you. This therefore is what I believe it means to offer yourselves as living sacrifices. Giving up (sacrificing) what I want to do with my life and giving it over to God's purpose for me. It doesn't mean doing God's will while secretly wishing I could be doing something else.

No wonder we have Christians everywhere saying, "I want to know and to do God's will for my life, but how do I find out what it is ? I always ask them, "Have you made your life a life of sacrifice as Paul instructs you to do in Romans 12: 1,2 ?" Never have I said that and had someone say, "Yes, I did that years ago and I still have no idea what it is that God wants me to do!" What they typically say is, "I never thought of those verses that way", and yet isn't that exactly what those two verses say? Well, let's move on. What else do we need to do to discover our ministry ?

Step 2 : Eliminate Competing Distractions

What about you - any distractions in your life ? Most of us would agree that in this world there are many, many distractions just waiting to take our minds off what is truly important. This is another reason why many Christians can't seem to come to grips with this whole idea of a personal ministry – they are continually distracted. Parenting, care-giving, work demands, television, radio, movies, print media, the internet, our own personal music selections following us around all day, intimate communication with friends and family, etc. etc., and all of that available instantly at our fingertips. We need some way to filter out what keeps us from making progress in our spiritual development. Deciding what is truly important and having the discipline not to allow these distractions to overwhelm our everyday lives; that's what is required from us. No wonder we are distracted! When all these issues have complete freedom to take over our attention and with no regard for what enters our minds; this is what helps to formulate what we think about and we can't help but only mark time in our Christian growth.

Step 3 : Evaluate My Strengths

We need some process to look carefully at our strengths, what we do well, instead of trying to evaluate **all** we do. Of all we do then, what does God really bless ?

Step 4: Cooperate with Other Believers

Development of the spiritual life is meant to be done in the company of other believers, not entirely on your own. I am **not** downplaying the value of solitude and getting off by yourself to listen to God speak to you without CD's, radio or books – just listening to God speak. One Christian writer says it this way, "If God wanted to say something to you, is your life quiet enough that you would be able to hear it?" I am saying that sometimes, perhaps the majority of the time, others can see in me ways that God is attempting to use me much more clearly than I can see that for myself. Cooperating with other believers simply means regularly putting yourself in the company of other like-minded souls in a small group setting that encourages real communication about the ways others might see you being used of God. Trust me; that process is likely to produce some really surprising results about how God is using or hopes to use you, if you will only try it.

Step 5: Activate Your Gifts (Your Spiritual Gifts that is)

The story is told of a young European girl who was given a piece of fine china on the occasion of each birthday or some other special event in her life. This went on for decades. When she finished college and was married, the boxes of china followed her into her new home and remained in the attic for years and years. For you see, in her mind, there was never an occasion special enough to open the boxes and actually use the china. After a lifetime, she passed away, and her children discovered the boxes of china which by now were worth many thousands of dollars, but they had never been used – the boxes never opened. "What joy they would have been to their mother and to others," they said, "if the boxes had just been opened!"

Thus it is with the Spiritual Gifts our Heavenly Father has given to us. For too many Christians, these gifts remain in their original boxes, never opened, never used. Discovering and activating my Spiritual Gifts is another way to discover my ministry, or that special way God intends to use me. More on this subject later.

So here it is, S.H.A.P.E., five ways, (perhaps not the only 5), that God uses to reveal His path for us. This is what this study is all about.

God gives us **S**piritual Gifts, He speaks directly to our **H**earts, He gives us skills and **A**bilities, He is the author of our wondrous **P**ersonalities, and He orchestrates the life **E**xperiences that come our way. Our response is to unwrap our Spiritual Gifts, monitor and listen closely to our heartbeats, discover and apply our skills and abilities, plug in our personalities and examine our life experiences. This is how to discover your ministry, your part in God's work in the world !

First, let's talk about Spiritual Gifts. There are ten truths about Spiritual Gifts which I would like to cover first.

1.Only believers have Spiritual Gifts – This is a subject for believers in Christ. The scripture in I Corinthians 2:14 says this :

*"**The man without the Spirit** does not accept the things that come from the Spirit of God, for they are foolishness to him, and he **cannot understand them,** because they are spiritually discerned." NIV*

If you don't believe this, try to engage a non-Christian in a discussion about Spiritual Gifts and you will find out just how difficult it is. Some authors say that Spiritual Gifts come to us at the moment of our conversion, at that instant when we give ourselves in surrender to the leadership of God's Holy

Spirit in our lives. Other theologians say that the Spiritual Gifts are always there, they just emerge when we make this decision. Whether or not they are gifted to us at the time of our conversion or they are there at our birth and simply remain hidden in us until the moment of our conversion is not the important point. The important point is that only believers have them.

2.Every Christian has at least one Spiritual gift - I Corinthians 7 :7 says this :

*"But **each man** has his own gift from God; one has this gift, another has that." NIV*

It doesn't get any plainer than that.

3.No one receives all the gifts - I Corinthians 12: 27, 29-30:

*"Now you are the Body of Christ, and each one of you is a part of it. **Are all apostles** ? Are all prophets ? Are all teachers ? ....." NIV*

4.No single gift is given to everyone.

Again I Corinthians 12: 27, 29-30 Same as above

5.You can't earn or work for a Spiritual Gift Ephesians 4:7

*"But **to each one of us** grace has been given as Christ has apportioned it." NIV*

Spiritual Gifts are grace gifts from God. They cannot be earned or worked for.

6.The Holy Spirit decides what gifts I get - I Corinthians 12:11

*"All these are the work of one and the same Spirit, and **He gives to each man, just as He determines**."* *NIV*

The Holy Spirit decides what gift is appropriate for me. I don't get to choose what gift I like best or that I would prefer the gift of another.

7. The gifts I'm given are permanent   Romans 11: 29

*"For **God's gifts** and His call **are irrevocable**. "NIV*

This one is a surprise to many people. Most can quote the old adage, "If you don't use it, you lose it." However, Paul says in this passage, that God doesn't cast these gifts out to us like a bait waiting for a fish to strike. Then, if we don't use them in a certain time period, He jerks them back away from us. Instead, he pictures a patient father watching His gifted child acting in his own selfish interest and with this precious gift designed to be used for the Father's work, lying unopened.

Once while teaching this material in a medium security prison in rural North Carolina, I noticed a young man in the group of 23 inmates who sat in the back of the room with his arms crossed not taking part in the discussion. At the end of this presentation, he came forward and said to me, "Are you saying that these Spiritual Gifts are permanent and God doesn't jerk them away if you don't use them ?" I replied that the scripture appeared to me to say exactly that.

He then said to me, "Before I messed up my life and got sent here, I used to teach Bible Study in my church. I have already determined that when I got out of here, I would find a way to begin teaching the Bible again. But this passage says that God might have a use for me right here, teaching inside the walls of this prison. I don't have to wait until I get out of here. I can begin right now to be a witness for Him."

Yes, the gifts are permanent. Does that mean they never change? Yes and no. I believe that God continues to reveal to us new ways for us to be a witness for Him through the use of these gifts. But although these major areas of giftedness rarely disappear altogether, we use different gifts all the time, some with more effectiveness than others.

8. I am to develop the gifts God has given me -

I Timothy 4: 14

"Do not neglect your gift, *which was given to you through a prophetic message when the body of elders laid hands on you."* *NIV*

9.It's a sin to waste the gifts God gave me - I Corinthians 4: 2

*"Now it is required that those who have been given a trust **must prove faithful**. "NIV*

The KJV says :

*"Moreover, it is required in stewards that a man **be found faithful**." KJV*

What really does being found faithful mean? I would

submit to you that being found faithful means not only discovering your gift(s) but using them in a manner which meets the needs of those whom you encounter and points others to the God you serve and also to your Savior, Jesus, in whom you have placed your trust.

10. Using my gifts honors and glorifies God
John 15:8

*"This **is to my Father's glory** that you bear much fruit, showing yourselves to be my disciples." NIV*

When I use my gift(s), it not only pleases the Father but it gives Him glory and honor and says to others, ***this is the God I serve.***
And…..when I use my gift, it expands me.
I Chronicles 4: 10

*"Oh, that you would bless me **and enlarge my territory** ! Let Your hand be with me, and keep me from harm so that I will be free from pain." NIV*

This passage is better known as the prayer of Jabez. As I use my gift, it expands my influence with others and my horizons widen; I see more opportunities to use my gift(s), and the end result is, I am called upon to do more, serve more, all in His name.

In his letter to the church at Corinth, Paul says,

*"Now about Spiritual Gifts, **I do not want you to be ignorant."***   *I Corinthians 12: 1 NIV*

I don't want you to be ignorant ! In church after church, we find the same thing; Christians grossly ignorant about

Spiritual Gifts. Even pastors tell me they have not taught about this subject for many reasons; fear over the issue of tongues, fear that if a church member understands his or her gift he/she might demand the church allow them to use it immediately, fear and confusion over too many differing lists of Gifts to choose from – which list is correct? One pastor told me he thought his Spiritual Gift was humor. Another said his people expected him to have **all** the Spiritual Gifts equally! No wonder we slide away from this subject! Many national surveys have found that far less than 5% of Christians have any idea what Spiritual Gifts are, let alone what their Gift might be.

CHAPTER 3

S o let's move into this discussion of Spiritual Gifts and let's start with the best definition of a Spiritual Gift that I can come up with :

A Spiritual Gift is an endowment of motivation and ability, given by the Holy Spirit to every believer, to be used to minister to others and therefore build up the Body of Christ.

There's a lot here, so let's take it a piece at a time. First of all, a Spiritual Gift is an endowment, a supernatural endowment. It is a gift, an investment in you. Similar to an endowment to a university, it cannot be used up, it just keeps giving and growing. It is beyond my ability to understand or explain. I can't earn it. It is given to me by the Holy Spirit.

It is also a motivation, an inner desire to serve God in a certain way. Many times Christians say, "I ought to do this or I should do that." But, this says, "I must do it" ! This motivation that originates with my Spiritual Giftedness comes from the inside, not from the outside. We are used to being motivated from the outside; what we typically call motivation by guilt, or 'Christian arm twisting'. It goes something like this :"Go with me to the jail this week and

I promise I won't ask you again for at least a month !" Or, this, "I've asked you to go with me to the jail three times and you've always had something else to do." Motivation by GUILT ! Christian leaders frequently use the expression, "As a Christian, you **should**….. or **you ought to** …."

But, the use of a Spiritual Gift is different. Now, we are motivated from the inside, it's an assignment from God's Holy Spirit and we are compelled to do it. That's a big difference!

Finally, it is an ability, a special capacity to serve, which again originates with the Holy Spirit. As I said earlier, "God doesn't always choose those who are equipped, but He always equips those He chooses !" If God is calling you to serve, *He will* equip you.

So, there it is : What a plan ! I get the gift, the motivation or the desire to use the gift, and the ability to deliver the gift all in the same package ! Isn't God great !

The basic idea is this :

Will you live only for your own goals, comfort, and pleasure, or will you live the rest of your lives for God's glory, knowing that He has promised eternal rewards ?

> *"God has given to each of you from His great variety of Spiritual Gifts. Manage them well so that God's generosity can flow through you.*
> *I Peter 4: 10-11 NIV*

We bring God glory by worshipping Him, loving other believers, becoming like Christ, serving others with our gifts, and telling others about Him.

It's so confusing; just what **are** the Spiritual Gifts ? It's very difficult to teach a subject that doesn't stand still. By that I mean that there's almost as many lists of Spiritual Gifts as there are authors. Every time I pick up a book on the subject, it seems like I find a new list. It appears that scripture just isn't very clear on this subject. Here's the only way I know to present this subject. We need to focus on **using** our gifts for God's purposes rather than spending our time trying to discover the **real** list of Spiritual Gifts, because I'm not sure there is a real list. So, for the purposes of this discussion, I will show you a number of Spiritual Gift lists. You may choose the list you prefer and I will not argue with you. I will tell you what my list is and why I have chosen it but, again, you are free to choose any list you wish. If you write me or see me in person and plead your case to me to include your gift on my list, I will gently remind you of this discussion, but I might ask this question, "How does God use you and your gift of….?" In other words, the focus of any discussion of Spiritual Gifts ought not to be on what they are but rather on how God is using that gift through you. Amen ? So, with that introduction, let's begin. I'm going to show you different lists of Spiritual Gifts from different authors.

Here's Spiritual Gift list #1. Note that it has 20 items. This author has neatly arranged them into categories for us : The Ministry of Helping, the Ministry of Directing Others, and the Ministry of the Word. For want of a better description, the last category is called the Ministry of the Spectacular ! In list #1 therefore, Miracles are a Spiritual Gift, as are Music, Evangelism and 'Healings'.

List #1 *(20 items)*

Ministry of Helping
√ Serving
√ Giving
√ Showing Mercy
√ Craftsmanship
√ Healings

Ministry of Directing Others
√ Leadership
√ Faith

Ministry of the Word
√ Apostleship   √ Wisdom   √ Prophecy
√ Knowledge   √ Evangelism √ Music
√ Discernment of spirits   √ Pastor-teacher
√ Teaching   √ Exhortation

Ministry of the Spectacular
√ Miracles   √ Tongues   √ Interpretation of tongues

38

List #2 has only 9 items.

List # 2 *(9 items)*

√ Apostle   √ Healing
√ Prophet   √ Helps
√ Teacher   √ Government
√ Evangelist   √ Diversity of Tongues
√ Miracle Worker

39

Healing is listed again as is Evangelist and Miracle Worker.

List #3 also has 9 items but they are a different 9. These are actual lists from different authors.

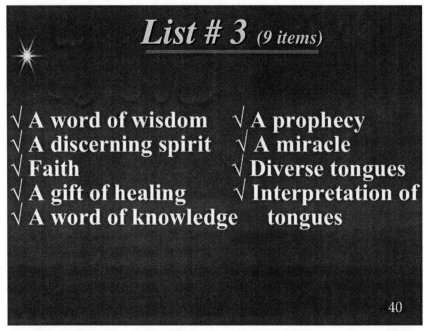

List # 3 *(9 items)*

√ A word of wisdom
√ A discerning spirit
√ Faith
√ A gift of healing
√ A word of knowledge
√ A prophecy
√ A miracle
√ Diverse tongues
√ Interpretation of tongues

40

The following list came from a church where I made this presentation. When I arrived on Friday afternoon, they had each table decorated in the Fellowship Hall with small packages representing each of the Spiritual Gifts. I had never seen this list before. In order to make them feel more comfortable with my presentation, I added this list to my presentation. Where they got the list, I do not know.

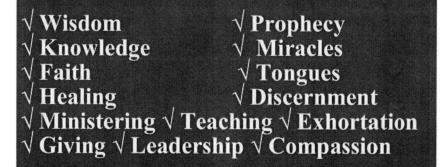

List # 4 *(14 items)*

√ Wisdom   √ Prophecy
√ Knowledge   √ Miracles
√ Faith   √ Tongues
√ Healing   √ Discernment
√ Ministering √ Teaching √ Exhortation
√ Giving √ Leadership √ Compassion

41

List #5 is interesting. It comes from a book called, <u>The Three Colors of Ministry</u> by Christian Schwarz. I was struck by the sheer number of Spiritual Gifts identified by the author.

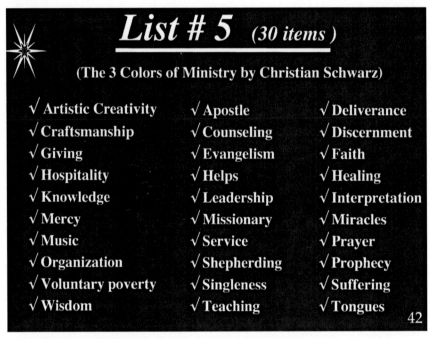

List # 5 *(30 items)*

(The 3 Colors of Ministry by Christian Schwarz)

√ Artistic Creativity	√ Apostle	√ Deliverance
√ Craftsmanship	√ Counseling	√ Discernment
√ Giving	√ Evangelism	√ Faith
√ Hospitality	√ Helps	√ Healing
√ Knowledge	√ Leadership	√ Interpretation
√ Mercy	√ Missionary	√ Miracles
√ Music	√ Service	√ Prayer
√ Organization	√ Shepherding	√ Prophecy
√ Voluntary poverty	√ Singleness	√ Suffering
√ Wisdom	√ Teaching	√ Tongues

42

He lists 30 items, some of which are quite fascinating. For instance, Craftsmanship. The author says that in the Old Testament, God says in Exodus 31: 3,

> *"I (God)....have given him skill, ability, and knowledge in all kinds of crafts..."* NIV

What about Voluntary Poverty ? Plenty of people could be judged to be living in poverty, but not many have chosen Voluntary Poverty, and fewer yet would identify it as a Spiritual Gift. And Singleness. Plenty of people live as singles, yet identifying it as a Spiritual Gift seems strange. Where does the author get these gifts ? The concepts are discussed in the scriptures, but they are not described anywhere in the Scriptures as Spiritual Gifts. The author says his list does not come specifically from Scripture, but rather from his 30 plus years as a pastor where he has seen these gifts illuminated in the lives of his people. If we are going to take that route to identifying Spiritual Gifts, we will never agree on any specific list. So, I offer my previous words to you again : let's not focus so much attention on what the gifts **are**, but rather on how God is using you and your gift no matter how you choose to describe it.

I would rather take another route. Let me show you list #6, my list. It comes from the 12th. chapter of Romans, verses 6 through 8; here it is :

What Are the Spiritual Gifts ?

Taft's List from Romans 12: 6-8 :

- **Prophecy** - Proclaiming God's truth
- **Serving** - Meeting practical need
- **Teaching** - Clarifying truth from scripture
- **Exhortation** - Encouraging the faith of others
- **Giving** - Losing yourself in the needs of others
- **Ruling** - Providing leadership or standing before
- **Mercy** - Pity plus acting on the needs of others 43

There they are : Prophecy, Serving, Teaching, Exhortation, Giving, Ruling (or Leadership) and Mercy (or Compassion). So, for the purposes of this discussion, I will focus on **this** list, and then at the conclusion, I will spend a few minutes telling you why I have chosen it. It is the same list used by James Mahoney in his book, Journey Into Usefulness. Many of my descriptive comments about Spiritual Gifts are taken from this very well written and life-changing book.

I. The Spiritual Gift of Prophecy, or speaking for God. The use of this Spiritual Gift reveals righteous and unrighteous motives or actions by presenting God's truth. These people are persuasive in speech. They reveal secrets of men's, hearts and cause them to fall down and worship God. The object is to hear God's voice. This gift is not so much about 'foretelling' the future as it is about 'forth telling' God's word. It comes from the Hebrew word 'navi' and the Greek word 'prophetes' which means to speak on behalf of another; a prophet speaks for God. Usually what they have to say is on the basis of what they have learned of Him in the Scriptures. Some claim a direct 'Hot Line' to heaven, "God told me….", but I have become somewhat leery of this line. The more forceful someone is in telling me that they have heard directly from God, the more I tend to back away. Now I believe God **can** give you specific instruction for yourself or someone else, but these times are rare and subject to gross misuse and should not be used casually. The Prophets are not concerned in the slightest if you are offended by their words. They believe that the words which offend you are not their words, they are the words of God. Furthermore, if you need proof of that, they can point you to the Scriptures that say just that. Bottom line: Prophets are not concerned with popularity. If that's what one strives to achieve, this is definitely not his or her gift. In fact, that is not the goal of any of the gifts. The goal with all the gifts is to use them for God's glory and not our own.

Here's how to test yourself if you believe you might have the Spiritual Gift of Prophecy :

- Do you long to tell your story to others ?
- How intense is your motivation to speak for God ? Is it to be heard or to tell ? Some people just have a need to be heard. This is a different need : To tell about the way God loves each of us and desires only the best for us.
- Are you willing to commit your life to the exercising of this gift ? This question can be asked of any Spiritual Gift. Every Spiritual Gift is backed by a lifetime commitment to use it for His glory.
- If you have experienced opportunities to speak for God, did the results verify your gift ? Did things happen which took God to explain ? Were lives transformed ? (i.e., is God speaking through you) ?

II. The Spiritual Gift of **Serving**. This is simply detecting the personal needs of others and demonstrating love by meeting those needs. People who exercise this gift overlook their own personal discomfort. The server has genuine affection for others, demonstrates brotherly responsibility, and is always willing to let others take credit. The object is to meet needs. These people are truly 'hooked on service.' They render sacrificial and effective service to others — they are doers. The Holy Spirit opens the eyes of servers to practical ways of meeting human need and they are drawn to it like metal to a magnet, where others pass by unaffected. I confess that I am really good at seeing need and passing right by it without stopping in order to meet commitments already decided upon. The thing is, we're not just talking about needs which we see and basically ignore; we're talking about needs which many of us don't even see. Those with the Spiritual Gift of Serving see those needs and race to meet them, sometimes before those they are serving even know they have a need ! That's the Spiritual Gift of Serving.

My wife has this gift and it is truly amazing to watch at times. For instance, we will attend a dinner at the church together and after it is over, we will be walking out the door when I will notice she is no longer next to me. I turn around and automatically, I know where she is. I find her in the kitchen cleaning up a few dishes left over or wiping down tables with a few others. If you ask her what are you doing ? She will answer, "I'm helping to clean up." If you then say, "Were you asked to do that ?", she will answer, "No, **it just needed to be done**."

Here's how to test yourself for this gift :

- When it comes to helping people, are you a doer – do you have a restless urge to do something about the needs of the world ?
- Must people coax you into helping or is your response to tasks spontaneous ? Those with this gift are often embarrassed when others point out a need that they have not seen. Those with the Spiritual Gift of Service feel they should have seen it before anyone else. And one other thing : It's very difficult to praise servers. They do not want the praise of others and certainly not in public. Remember the goal : meeting needs, not praise.
- Do you accept this gift as your basic service responsibility?

Do others see it in you ? Do they see God acting through you ?

•Do you find lasting satisfaction through your service ? Does God bless through it ?

III. The Spiritual Gift of **Teaching**. Those with the Spiritual Gift of Teaching search out and validate truth – God's truth. They engage in research and detailed study in order to validate truth. They must be diligent in detail, fervent in spirit, and do his or her work with the Lord's work on earth in mind.

The object is changed lives, not enjoyment. Many people approach teachers and pastors with comments such as, "I really enjoyed your teaching or preaching." Most pastors and teachers have learned to be polite over the years by responding with the politically correct, "Thank you".....or, "The praise goes to the Lord." However, inside, they are thinking, "This is **not** entertainment. Why are these people saying, I enjoyed it ?" A real compliment to a teacher or preacher will focus on the changing of lives, which **is** the goal. Even though most preachers and teachers do enjoy what they do it is still a good idea to remember that the next time you wish to pay a compliment to a teacher or preacher.

The Spiritual Gift of Teaching brings special illumination for scripture like roadway reflectors showing the way on a foggy night. My wife and I own a home in the North Carolina mountains, just off the Blue Ridge Parkway. I cannot tell you the number of times we have traveled up the mountain from Charlotte in dense fog with nothing to guide us except the reflectors in the middle of the road. That's the way scripture is for teachers. Certain scriptural passages shine like reflectors, calling attention to themselves, saying, "Tell them this" or, "make sure they see the meaning here." This Spiritual Gift is evidenced by illuminated interpretation, systematic searching, and clear communication. These people relish opportunities to teach biblical truth. *They seek out these opportunities; they just don't respond when people ask.* Their teaching is clear, forceful and compelling. What good would it do if biblical truth were presented and it wasn't clear, or the presenter couldn't articulate or find the right words to communicate his or her message ?

Finally, the message must be compelling, meaning something must be done about what I just heard. It isn't good enough just to hear about the way God would have me live my life; I must change and reprioritize my life as a result of what I've heard.

To test for the Spiritual Gift of Teaching, ask these questions :

- ■Do you have a hunger for scripture and insight into its meaning and are those insights exciting to share ?
- ■Do you study the Bible more than other Christians around you ? Do you have a number of resource books which you use regularly ?
- ■Are the lives of others affected by your gift and do they affirm this gift in you ?

One young man came up to me after this presentation and told me he frequently woke up around 5:00 or 5:30 AM on Sunday morning and couldn't go back to sleep, so he would get up and go out to his desk and work on his Sunday School lesson. Sometime later, his wife would come out and say, "What are you doing ?" He replied, "I'm just doing some more work on my lesson." She looked at the five or six reference books he had laying open on his desk and his lesson notes which were four pages long and said, "Don't you think you already have enough to present ? Besides, you often tell me you can't get through all the material you have anyway." He said to me, "She thinks there's something wrong with me. Am I crazy ?" I said, "No, you're not crazy. You're just a Teacher – that's what the Spiritual Gift of Teaching looks like."

IV. The Spiritual Gift of **Exhortation** or **Encouragement**. Those with this Spiritual Gift stimulate the faith of others. They engage in personal counseling to encourage spiritual growth. They call to the side to encourage a course of action. Exhorters rejoice in hope, are patient with slow progress and are persistent in prayer. The object is the deepened faith of others. Exhortation comes from the Greek word "parakaleo" or to call to one's side – 'come sit by my side' is the picture that we see. If this is your main gift, you will begin to love enough to be personally involved in the lives of others and you will care enough to comfort others in a very personal manner.

You may test for this gift by asking the following questions :

- Do you have a deep desire for God to touch the lives of others through you ?
- Does God seem to give you a 6th. sense of when to act or to speak or a personal touch with people which motivates them to action ?
- Do others consistently seek you out for counsel or help?

The Spiritual Gift of Exhortation (Encouragement)

was brought clearly into focus one day as I listened to a friend tell how a typical day went in her life. She said she was frequently asked for advice on all kinds of issues on a daily basis. When she went to the grocery store or to Target, often she would have an encounter in the shopping aisle or in the check out lane where she was called upon to pray with someone who was struggling with a serious life or relationship issue. Her husband would get irritated because this happened so frequently. He would go to the car and fume while he waited. She told of how she would overhear a conversation between a lady and the checkout clerk about how terrible the day had gone so far. She said, "I would lean over, apologize for overhearing the conversation and then ask if I might pray with her over by the return desk." She told me she didn't understand why this happened to her until my presentation and then the light came on as she recognized how God was using her in this way. Now, when it happens and her husband is nearby, he simply whispers, "I'll be in the car, praying for you as you encourage this woman !"

This just doesn't happen to everyone. But, almost every time I relate this story, I frequently have people say to me, "Yes, you're right. It doesn't happen to everyone, but it happens to me too."

A lady in Alaska came up to me after the presentation on a Saturday evening and told me how much she resented her husband counseling those in their church and she had thought about leaving him because of it. She told me he left early most mornings to have breakfast with someone who needed his word, and then many evenings, he would invite someone who was struggling with an important issue over to the house just to talk. "When we go to a church function," she said, "he is always the last to leave and when I go to look for him, he will be quietly speaking with someone who asked him for help." She told me with tears flowing down her face,

"This is the first time I have ever thought about the fact that God might be using him this way. He is always encouraging me in my job – I just always assumed he didn't want to be around me and I felt neglected because of the time he spent with others. Now, I understand and I pray for him when he is exercising his wonderful gift of encouragement."

One woman, well known in Baptist circles in North Carolina, expresses her Spiritual Gift of Encouragement during her working days this way : She mails your prior year's Christmas card back to you perhaps in April or in June with a new message of encouragement and a personal prayer for you that day.

Another woman in our church spends hundreds of dollars sending personal cards to dozens of church members for birthdays, those who are ill or recuperating from surgery or those she hasn't seen in a while at worship. Newcomers to our church are astounded at her faithfulness. These kind of actions are not carried out by accident – they are examples of God working through the Spiritual Gift of Encouragement.

V. The Spiritual Gift of **Giving**. Those with this gift entrust their personal assets to others for the furtherance of their ministries. They organize their personal business in order to gain assets. They possess an ability to make quick decisions regarding the immediate needs of others. The giver must give freely to the total needs of Christians and take a genuine interest in the needs of strangers. The object again is meeting needs. From the Greek word "metadidomi" which means more than a mere contribution, but rather a giving or a 'pouring out of self' which sometimes astonishes others. Paul himself speaks of this in his letter to the church at Philippi in chapter 2, verse 17, when he says,

"But even if I am being poured out like a

drink offering…..” NIV

Paul's words form a word picture as if he is opening a valve on his side and all his life's energy is being poured out in sacrifice and service. That's the way this gift is presented. It's an ability to lose yourself in a reckless abandon for others caused by the Holy Spirit moving in your life. This is truly heroic type action that goes far above and beyond the call of duty. It **can** be about giving financially. However, it is also about giving of self. Many Christians with the Spiritual Gift of Giving mistake it simply for service. When viewed more closely, however, this service is really the Spiritual Gift of Giving due to the extent and completeness of that service.

Asking these questions can help identify this Spiritual Gift :

- Do you often find yourself giving more than others – of your resources and of yourself ?
- Are others often amazed at the extent of your giving ?
- When involved in Christian service, are you usually the first to arrive, the last to leave and the least likely to quit ?
- Does God seem to require more of you ?

One young man told me that during this S.H.A.P.E. presentation one week-end, his wife leaned over to him and said, "That sounds like you." "I had to admit, it did," he told me later. "I was thinking the same thing," he said. Now he is convinced that God does use him and his Spiritual Gifts of Giving and Leadership. Every year the corporation he represents sends him and his wife on a company-paid vacation to some exotic location as a reward for meeting pre-set sales goals. Now when they go, he checks in advance for mission opportunities such as orphanages, hospitals and other mission sites where they can make a difference. Then he communicates with the rest of the group and asks them to bring items that are needed including cash. When they arrive at their destination, he delivers the items using several rented vans along with a check to an astonished administrator. He tells of delivering two van loads of school supplies such as crayolas, pens, pencils, chalk, writing tablets and other needed supplies along with two air conditioners and a water purification unit plus a check for $2000 on just one such trip. He said, "Just think about this. There are school children in Puerto Rico with chalk and pencils, drinking clean water because of the ripple effect of your teaching on Spiritual Gifts and my response to that teaching." He and his wife give 10 % of the profits of their corporation each year to charitable causes as well. "Before I knew of my Spiritual Gift, we just went on the trip. Now we go and we give. It's such a wonderful feeling knowing God is using me in this way."

VI. The Spiritual Gift of **Ruling or Leadership**. This Gift coordinates the activities of others for the common good. They preside over; they lead and stand before. They are able to distinguish major objectives from the minor ones and help others to visualize them also. They readily bless those who curse them and do whatever they can to make their life spiritually prosperous. The object is moving God's people forward. From the Greek word "proistamenos" or to stand before, to preside over. The one thing that sets the leader apart is a sense of divine authority for the task. This is how I believe God works in spiritual leadership. I believe it is two fold :

> 1st. If God has chosen you, He will move in the hearts of others and lead you to them.
>
> 2nd. But...he will always validate that selection by issuing a personal call to you. I have experienced this call to leadership personally and I can assure you it is not just in the imagination.

These are the individuals in your churches who, for example, calmly stand up at a business meeting where an important and complex issue is being discussed and say something like this, "Folks, I've been listening to this discussion and it looks to me to be quite simple. First, we need to take care of this issue by Friday. Then, by the end of this month, we need to do so and so. Finally, these last two issues can wait until the next budget is put together." As you look around the room, people are nodding their heads and saying things like, "That makes a lot of sense, why didn't I think of that ?" The church quickly votes on that course of action and moves on.

You can test for the Spiritual gift of Ruling (Leadership) by asking the following questions :

- Have you ever felt a 'call' to lead out in some Christian endeavor ? Do others consistently look to you and ask for your leadership ?
- Has God verified His call to you by leading others to you ?
- Are you the kind of person who could organize a tornado?
- Has Satan ever opposed you in your effort ?

This last point is a real issue for those who would have the courage to lead others in spiritual matters. Satan, or the powers of evil, or however you choose to say it, is quite comfortable with you attending church on a regular basis, giving a modest offering, singing the hymns, listening to the sermon, even commenting on the sermon later. However, when you stand and offer spiritual leadership while others continue to sit, you get the full attention of the evil one. For those who would lead in this way, make sure you have all the doors of your spiritual and moral house closed and locked, for those same forces of evil will be 'reading your game tapes,' looking for an open door to ruin the very leadership you are offering – a sobering thought for those with the Spiritual Gift of Ruling (Leadership).

VI. The Spiritual Gift of Showing **Mercy or Compassion**. Those with this Spiritual Gift can identify and comfort those who are in distress. They mentally and emotionally relate to those who are experiencing misery or misfortune and give them aid. The merciful must share the happiness of those who are happy and enter into the sorrow of those who are sorrowful. The object is to offer comfort. There are people whom you know that are always first at the home where a loved one has been lost. They don't stand around and say, "What can I do?" They might say instead, "Where is your vacuum cleaner, I'll get this dirt up around the front door," or, "Let me get this trash out of the kitchen; where is your trash can ?" or, "I know your son is coming this afternoon by plane; what time is his flight arriving – may I pick him up at the airport?" They seem to know exactly what to say or to do in a situation like that.

From the Greek word "eleos" or to feel sympathy with the misery of another and manifests itself in action – yours! This is caring at a really deep level – beyond being willing to be inconvenienced, beyond being personally involved and helping, but seeing other's pain as your pain, their need as your need, their sorrow as your sorrow – this is not natural for anyone to care like that. I am willing to be inconvenienced on occasion. I am willing to become personally involved at times and even help out. Caring in the manner of this gift is far past me.

Testing for the Spiritual Gift of Mercy (Compassion) means asking questions like these :

- Do you actually feel the pain and need of others and do you respond ?
- Do you seem to care more than others ?
- Do others recognize this gift in you ?
- Is your first response at an automobile accident scene to get help or to tend to those who are hurt ? The merciful are most inclined to do the latter.

These are the seven areas in which God will supernaturally gift you. You must be willing to 'sell out' to the use of your Spiritual Gift. You must consider this gift "a pearl of great value' and worth sacrificing all of your natural talents and abilities in using it. The key question is this : If the Lord returns tomorrow, will He find you using your gift?

CHAPTER 4

So why the confusion ? The best answer I can find is this : Some Christian writers have observed that the confusion is caused by mixing up the gifts themselves (enablements), with the ways the gifts are used (ministries/roles), and the effects the gifts have upon others when they are exercised (manifestations).

Take a look at I Corinthians 12: 4 NIV, Paul says this :

"There are different kinds of spiritual gifts but the same Spirit.

The Greek word he uses for gifts is "charismaton", the same word he uses in Romans 12: 6-8 when he talks about Spiritual Gifts and lists them: Prophesying, Serving, Teaching, Exhorting, Giving, Ruling and Mercy. This is why I have chosen this list.

But let's move on, In verse 5 of this same passage, Paul goes on, *"There are different kinds of service, but the same Lord."* The Greek word he uses here is "diakonion", from which we get the word Deacon or service. This is the same Greek word he uses in I Corinthians 12, verse 28, where he supposedly presents another list of "Spiritual Gifts", but now we see he is actually referring to roles or ministries people are engaged in such as Apostle, Prophet, Teacher, Miracle Worker, Healer, Helper, Administrator, and Speakers of Diverse Tongues.

Finally, he declares in verse 6, *"There are different kinds of working, but the same God works all of them in all men."* The Greek word he uses here is "energematon", from which we get the word operations, effects or manifestation. He goes on immediately to list those effects as : a word of wisdom, a word of knowledge, faith, healing, miracles, prophecy, discerning spirits, speakers of different tongues, and interpreters of those different tongues. So, obviously, if we mix up all these different Greek words, we can come up with multiple lists of Spiritual Gifts. But, if we stick with the Greek word "charasmaton", we are left with the list in Romans 12: 6-8.

Let's consider what I call the Billy Graham analogy again from James Mahoney's life-changing book, <u>Journey Into Usefulness</u>. Most would agree with the idea that Graham has the Spiritual Gift of Prophecy, or speaking for God. He exercises that Spiritual Gift in his **role** as an evangelist. Evangelism isn't the Spiritual Gift, but rather the role he is in at that time. And what results is a word of wisdom. Now wisdom isn't the Spiritual Gift, but rather the manifestation or effect of Graham exercising his Spiritual Gift of Prophecy.

We can create another example, using Billy Graham and the Spiritual Gift of Exhortation. He exercises this Spiritual Gift in his **role** as a teacher. In this case, teaching isn't the Spiritual Gift but a role Graham is in. What results is increased faith in someone listening to him. Again, faith isn't the Spiritual Gift; it is the manifestation or the **effect** of Graham exercising his Spiritual Gift of Exhortation. I have experienced this in my own church. Not every Sunday School teacher exhibits the Spiritual Gift of Teaching. Those Sunday School teachers with the Spiritual Gift of Compassion, for example, interrelate with those who come on Sunday morning with much deeper sensitivity on Sunday and through the week than say someone with the Spiritual Gift of Teaching. In fact, I believe that those with a strong sense of the Spiritual Gift of Teaching must be careful to involve the Spiritual Gifts of others in the administration of a Sunday School class in order to balance other critical issues like : Welcoming visitors, contacting members through the week, care for the class members experiencing a life crisis and outreach and mission efforts, all of which *may* be neglected by the one with the Spiritual Gift of Teaching.

That is the best attempt I can give to why there is so much confusion about exactly what the Spiritual Gifts are. I have found two authors who agree with this view. They are : James Mahoney, in the already mentioned, <u>Journey Into Usefulness</u> and Don and Katie Fortune in their book : <u>Discovering Your God-Given Gifts</u>. And to quote Mahoney,

> "And this is where the water hits the wheel in terms of mobilizing our full Christian work force. The key to productive Christian service is for each and every Christian to discover his (or her) Spiritual Gift for service, determine how God would have him (or her) *exercise* it, and verify it by its *effect* in the lives of others.....as a part of God's redemptive purpose in the world."

Remember, the purpose of Spiritual Gifts is not for my benefit, but for the benefit of others. It is to bring maturity and harmony to the church family. If that is not the case, proceed with caution, or stop altogether. A pastor once told me of someone in his church who came to him and demanded that since he had the Spiritual Gift of teaching, he must be immediately assigned a teaching responsibility in the church. This is an example of a Spiritual Gift from an immature Christian producing disharmony, exactly the opposite of what is intended. You should also recognize that you have both a primary and a secondary ministry in your church. Your primary ministry should be in the area where you are Spiritually Gifted. Your secondary ministry includes serving in any other area of the body where you are needed. For example, if the youth of the church are sponsoring a car wash in order to raise funds for a mission trip and you are approached to contribute, it would be inappropriate to say, "I don't have the Spiritual Gift of Giving, so I will not contribute." If you have the funds, give ! Or how about this example ? A young man noticed a woman enter the sanctuary before worship. As she sat down in the pew next to him, she begin to weep softly. He touched her gently on the shoulder and said, "I have the Spiritual Gift of Teaching, but if you will wait here for just a moment, I will find someone with the Spiritual Gift of Mercy and they should be able to help you. !" No, that's not how it works. Sometimes you just have to do the best you can with what you've got !

There are at least six cautions about Spiritual Gifts that I would mention :
1. Don't confuse Spiritual Gifts with natural talents.
   a. For example : Singing is a natural talent or ability, but when another hears God speaking through your singing, that is a Spiritual Gift (i.e. Prophecy)

46

b.Public speaking is a natural talent or ability, but when another is encouraged through your spoken word, that is a Spiritual Gift (i.e. Exhortation)

2. Don't confuse Spiritual Gifts with the Fruit of the Spirit found in Galatians 5: 22-23. The Fruit of the Spirit refers to those qualities of your life which appear when you allow more and more control of your life to be turned over to God's Holy Spirit. For example, I have always been amused by the refrigerator magnet which reads, "Lord, I want patience, and I want it right now !" Patience is one of the Fruits of the Spirit which occur in my life when I turn over more control to God's Holy Spirit. It is a *result* of my Christian maturity, not something I can gain by asking for it. Over time, I should be able to see the Fruit of the Spirit (like patience, for example) growing in my life. Therefore, "Fruit" shows or points toward my maturity in Christ and "Gifts" show or point toward my Ministry.

3. Don't confuse gifts with Christian roles. We have already discussed this in the previous section. Evangelist and Pastor are not Spiritual Gifts in my view. Again, I reiterate the point made at the beginning of the discussion on Spiritual Gifts. If we disagree on exactly what the gifts are or on how we might describe them, that's ok. The important thing is that God desires to use me and my gift no matter how I choose to describe it.

4. Be aware of the gift projection tendency; that is expecting others to serve the way you do and to achieve the same results. We hear comments like, "Why didn't you see that

need and/or do something about it – I did !" That's what is called 'gift projection'. I once had another Deacon in our church tell me that family ministry was easy; anyone could do it. Just send a few cards throughout the year, contact the family periodically and make sure to remember birthdays and other special events like anniversaries. I told him that teaching my Bible study class was easy for me also. He responded by saying, "That's totally different – you have to be gifted for that !" I don't believe he ever got my point. I believe you have to be gifted to do any ministry well including the Deacon Family Ministry, but that's another subject.

5. Don't feel that your Spiritual Gift makes you, in any way, superior to others. The scripture teaches us that all the gifts are equal and necessary for the body to function properly. In I Corinthians 12: 21 Paul says,

> *"The eye cannot say to the head, 'I don't need you!' And the head cannot say to the feet, 'I don't need you!'. NIV*

Some of the Spiritual Gifts have speaking roles (Prophecy, Teaching, Exhortation, Ruling or Leadership) and some do not. Some believe the speaking gifts are more important. Scripture however, does not support that view. All are needed; all are necessary.

6. And finally, realize that using your Spiritual Gift without love is worthless.

Paul again tells us in I Corinthians 13:1-3

> *"If I speak with the tongues of men and of angels, but have not love, I am only a resounding gong or a clanging cymbal. If I have the gift of prophecy, and can*

fathom all mysteries and all knowledge, and if I have a faith that can move mountains, but have not love, I am nothing. If I give all I possess to the poor and surrender my body to the flames, but have not love, I gain nothing."
NIV

Many times this passage is used in wedding ceremonies to speak of the love between a man and a woman. Paul uses this beautiful language differently. Paul uses it to illustrate the motivation behind the exercising of Spiritual Gifts just discussed previously in I Corinthians 12. According to Paul, the only acceptable motivation for using Spiritual Gifts is love – unconditional love.

CHAPTER 5

Another powerful quote from Dr. Edge came to me personally : "Some church members", he said, "have a commitment level which leads them to be loyal in **attending** the institutional meetings of the church and even in meeting some of the needs of fellow church members, yet…they are unwilling to give the time and energy to become seriously involved with those who are hurting and broken outside the walls of the church". How do we motivate people to go to the marketplace with their faith ?" Dr. Edge seems to be saying that the church has emphasized **coming** so much to its people, that for many, **coming** becomes the goal ! We **come** to church, and we even meet the needs of some who are part of our church community, but for the majority of church members, we are not involved with Jesus' redemptive message of 'Being Good News' (Ministry) and 'Telling Good News' (Evangelism), outside the walls of the church. Our churches then re-enforce that view by ignoring Jesus' redemptive call as well. How **do** we motivate people to go to their marketplace with their faith ?

Here's another quote from author and church consultant, North Carolina's own, Eddie Hammett :

"Eight million adults who were active churchgoers as teenagers will no longer be active in a church by the time they reach 30."

How about this one ?

"Since 1991, the adult population in the United States has grown by 15%. During the same period the number of adults who do not attend church has nearly doubled, a 92% increase !"

What must take place is a fundamental rethinking of just what the Christian church's mission is all about. As Rick Warren says, **"It is not about you**; it is about God and **His** work in the world."** That** is what the church is to be about. It's not about coming; it's about going – going out into a world that is hurting and crying out to know the One who guides your life – this Jesus whom you claim to worship.

Let's be clear. God calls you to a life changing relationship with Him through Jesus Christ, His Son. Author Randy Singer puts it this way : "Churches are filled with good people who live nice lives but fail to have this personal relationship with the one who designed them". Coming to church is unquestionably a part of that relationship. But it isn't the only part. My relationship with Christ doesn't end at church; that's where it begins. One prominent Christian leader has said that the biggest mission field the church has is inside its own walls.. If Christians truly believe that their response to the invitation God gives to participate with Him in bringing his creation back into fellowship with Him is to **come** to church, then the church is in serious trouble indeed.

Let's continue with our discussion about Spiritual Gifts.

The best two references I have found on this subject are : James Mahoney's book, <u>Journey Into Usefulness</u> published in the mid 70's, by Broadman Press. Although this book is no longer available over the retail counter, I have had no problem finding it in the various rare book sites on the Internet at reasonable prices. This was truly a life-changing book for me personally decades ago when I first read it and many of my ideas on Spiritual Gifts have been either drawn from it or confirmed by it.

The second book entitled, <u>Discovering your God-Given Gifts</u> by Don and Katie Fortune has also been extremely helpful. The Fortunes agree with Mahoney in using the list of Spiritual Gifts or Enablements which Paul notes in Romans 12: 6-8. The Fortunes have also produced a youth version of their book, which, like the original, includes an instrument to help identify your Spiritual Gifts through a series of probing questions. You can find or help confirm your Spiritual Gift(s), by answering these questions, most productively in the presence of a small group.

Another way to find that special area that God has Gifted you is to experiment with different areas of service. In every community, there are dozens of agencies focused on meeting the specialized needs of groups of citizens. Choose one of these agencies and tell them of your desire to find that special place of service. Pick one that matches your area of interest and the times that you would be available to assist. Then give it a try. It doesn't have to be a lifetime commitment. You may want to try more than one. The important thing is that each area of involvement will give you more information about how God might desire to use you.

Another way to discover your Spiritual Gift is to request input from others. For many, it is easier for others to see how God is already using you or might use you, than it is for us to see that for ourselves. For this reason, I recommend to anyone studying this issue for themselves to pursue it in the presence of a small group. This is how I learned of my Giftedness decades ago and it is still a powerful method today. Outside of a small group, I tell seekers to go to those people in their lives who know you well and on whose judgment you trust. For most of us that number is small, usually just a few people. Meet with them over lunch or dinner. Ask them, "How do you see God trying to use me"? Then compare the answers with the input you are getting from your small group.

Sometimes it is easier to discover your gift through ministry rather than to discover your ministry through your gift. Let me explain. For many Christians, (I expect for most) it is easier to look at the things you are already doing in and through the church, and to search for the common threads that bind them together. After all, this is not an academic issue where we sequester ourselves in a conference room for a month or so and only come out after discovering our Spiritual Gift. For many of us, discovering our Spiritual Giftedness happens **as we are already serving**, not before we serve. Therefore, I always encourage someone to look at the areas of Christian service that bring you joy and look backwards to your Spiritual Gift. That is the most effective way I know of to find your Spiritual Gift.

There are three distinct ways God uses to guide us toward an understanding of our Spiritual Giftedness or the exercising of those Gifts.

I. Through an ongoing ministry. There are dozens of these ministries just waiting for you to become a part of their activity. Just call, set up an appointment and talk to them about volunteering for a short trial period.

II. Through a short term project. These projects are numerous and consist of a few hours on a certain day for clean up in a park, or alongside a highway, or some other worthwhile project to a week-end commitment such as leading a Deacon retreat, acting as a team member/leader on a Church Lay Renewal Week-end, or even something out of state. My wife and I have made several trips out of state from Alaska to Massachusetts to Idaho, teaching and leading Church Renewal events over just a few days each. Week-long commitments are also available through your local church or state missions organization. These range all over the block from a mission trip to an out of state site with a youth organization to even out of the country projects such as participation in the building of a seminary or teaching English in China. The key is this : You are setting the schedule, whether it be a few hours, a week-end, or a week-long commitment. It has a beginning, a middle, and an end point.

III. Through spontaneous situations. You can respond to one of these opportunities without even leaving your home or hometown. For example, members of the church youth group are selling car wash tickets to benefit their summer mission trip out of state. The men of the church are hosting a breakfast on Saturday morning to benefit their wheel chair ramp building project. Several low income children in the church cannot attend summer camp without additional financial support. A church member is in need of transportation to the hospital and didn't want to bother anyone to ask for help. An un-churched next door neighbor had an operation which has resulted in extensive rehabilitation and is in need of someone to go to the grocery store. The list goes on and on.

A good friend of mine introduced me to the concept of being pre-prayed when it comes to spontaneous situations. He said he was asked at a conference to lead a Bible study a few months out. He responded yes, he would do that. This immediate response astounded the man who had asked him. "Don't you want to pray about it?", he asked. My friend replied, "I pray each evening that God will send me opportunities tomorrow to use my gifts or to share my faith. So when you ask me to lead a Bible study, that's not something I need to pray about; that's an answer to prayer." Ever since hearing that story over 30 years ago, I have included that sentence in my prayer journal each day. Bring me opportunities to serve you tomorrow Lord and help me to have the good sense to recognize them when they appear.

There really are only three pre-requisites for finding your Spiritual Gift and here they are :

#1 Sacrifice : Only as you make a conscious decision to make your life a life of sacrifice to others, thereby centering yourself in His will for you -This takes us back to that passage in Romans 12 which was quoted earlier in verses 1 and 2. Anything else leaves you vulnerable to how you **feel** about using your gift on a day by day basis. This isn't about feeling. This is about finding that special place of service, committing yourself to action in that arena and then thanking

God as opportunities arise for you to use your gifts and abilities.

#2 Service : Only as you are already involved in meeting the needs of others -This isn't about sitting in a conference room and attempting to find that special place of service. This is about **doing, action – yours!** We've already covered this point as well. Remember, it is probably easier to find your gift **while already engaged** in some ministry than it is to find your ministry after an exhaustive study of your gifts.

#3 Self : Only as you give up trying to imitate the gifts of others – For years I thought there was a hierarchy of service in the church. I watched a good friend take on increasing levels of service and I decided to follow him. First he worked on various committees, then he chaired a committee and after that he chaired one of the four or five key church committees. Then he became a Deacon and then Chairman of the Deacons. I followed a year or two later. When I finally asked him about his service one day, he told me he, too, thought the way I did until one day he ran out of new assignments. He decided the only thing left must be to do them all over again. That's when he came to his senses. He told me that he had come to the conclusion that it wasn't about being on this committee or that committee or one committee being more important than the next or being Chair of the Deacons versus just being a Deacon. It was all about discovering how God had gifted him and how God intended to use him. We both discovered that through the Church Renewal Journey, and it has made all the difference. Both of us have the Spiritual Gift of leadership so we find ourselves being asked frequently to take a leadership role on this group or that. In addition, we both have the Spiritual Gift of Teaching so this is another area where we frequently find ourselves. This is the reason why I was so comfortable following him in service. However, his Leadership Gift is much stronger than mine and my Teaching Gift is more pronounced than his. Therefore, I am very comfortable with him in leadership roles which I have no intention of doing. Likewise, my teaching assignments are not something he would aspire to doing over time.

Here's another example. My good friend Marty Dupree is involved in training and promotion of Evangelism in the state of North Carolina. When Marty and his family moved into a neighborhood recently, *he and his wife* gave a block party for the other families on their cul-de-sac, not the other way around. He told me that way he could learn about them and something about their prayer concerns. Then when he jogs through his neighborhood, he prays for the families as he passes by their homes. He frequently prays for (and with) the server in busy restaurants at lunch when the food is delivered. His inquiry goes like this : "We're getting ready to pray about this food in just a moment. Is there a prayer request we could add for you as we do this ?" The response is usually quite positive and moving. When I learned these things about Marty and got to know him and the way he is always speaking out on behalf of his Lord, I became somewhat distressed. If I am so mature as a Christian, why wasn't I like Marty ? It gradually dawned on me that my responsibility was *not* to try to imitate Marty. My responsibility was to discover and be faithful to what God was trying to do *through me*. Perhaps that can be helpful to you as well.

There are other clues to discovering your Spiritual Gift. For example, out of all that you do as a Christian, what do you really enjoy ? I firmly believe that Christian service ought to be joyful and when it isn't, it's time to pause and ask why.

We met a young couple in Virginia at a Week-end and she told us that she was not very joyful about her service. She was the church organist/pianist and every church event she attended, like the Sunday School Christmas party, she was always asked to play the piano. She was kind and proceeded to play, but it took all the joy out of attending the event for her. She was tired of playing and took no joy from it at all. "I really want to teach," she said. I asked her, why she didn't just quit ? Then I thought to myself, this pastor will kill me when he finds out I gave her the idea. She told me she couldn't quit because there was no one to take her place. After I returned home, I received a letter from her. She had quit her job as church organist after a conversation with her pastor. He immediately inquired in the church newsletter if there was anyone interested in playing the organ in the worship service. Another lady came forward immediately and said she would love to do it. My friend said this is the best part. She and her husband were teaching a Sunday School class of young high school girls and loving every minute of it ! The joy of service had returned to her life !

Another good question to ask yourself is what does God really bless out of all that I do ? Most of us regular church-goers do a lot but what really stands out as being blessed by God ?

What do others encourage in me ? What do others see that God is trying to do through me that I might not see? I encourage you who struggle with this issue of "How does God want to use me ?" to meet with several Christian friends who know you well and whose judgment you trust and ask them, "What do you see in me that God may want to use ?"

What kind of inner leanings do you have ? What have you always thought about in the back of your mind as something you would like to do and that might prove useful to God's work in the world ?

What do you learn from your times of solitude, meditation, prayer and fasting ? I know what you are thinking. You're thinking he doesn't know that I don't have any of those times in my life. If you are like most Christian people I know, there's not much time for these faith disciplines. I confess. I am in the majority here. But that doesn't mean they are unimportant. This is the great secret of the Christian life. Sometimes God is most clear when we are quiet, but that seems to be increasingly difficult for many Christians. When the air around us gets quiet, we seem to feel we must fill it with something. Be still and know.

Before we leave the subject of Spiritual Gifts, two

additional points need to be made. The Fortunes, Don and Katie, did a survey of only a thousand individuals and their Spiritual Gifts, but the result is interesting.

Frequency of Gifts $n=1000$

◆ Perceiver	12 %
◆ Server	17 %
◆ Teacher	6 %
◆ Exhorter	16 %
◆ Giver	6 %
◆ Administrator	13 %
◆ Mercy	30 %

87

If the Spiritual Gifts were equally divided, you would expect to find ~14% in each category. That's about the case with 4 of the Gifts but notice Teacher (and Giver) at only 6% each. It brings to mind the passage in James 3 where he says, "Not many of you should act as teachers, my brothers, because you know that we who teach will be judged more strictly!" And what about the 30% listed for Compassion (or Mercy) ? Do you think it could have anything to do with how much Mercy/Compassion is needed in today's world ? Now, to be clear, I do not know if these percentages would hold with a higher number of participants, but it is interesting.

Finally, we come to an idea Findley Edge recited where he outlines generally, **where** Spiritual Gifts are exercised. He says, that some, perhaps as many as 20% of us, will find the main expression of our gifts in and/or through the church; maybe not one specific church, but perhaps in many churches. It is not difficult to see where the gifts could be exercised in the church – Teaching Special Bible Studies, or teaching on Sunday morning, preaching, serving anywhere there is need, etc.

For a few, perhaps 15%, will find the expression of their gifts where society is hurting – Meals on Wheels, tax preparation for the elderly, Big Brother or Big Sister Programs, ministry to unwed mothers, etc.

An even smaller group (~5%), Findley says, will find their place of ministry in the Structures of Society, such as serving on the City Council or State Government, or as a judge in the court system, or perhaps serving in the Criminal Justice system as a Police Officer or Highway patrolman, or sitting on a board controlling the placement of individuals for public housing such as a member of my church did for years.

But for the majority of us (perhaps as many as 60%), Findley suggests we will find our place of ministry where we spend most of our waking hours – i.e. at work or in the home. For all these groups, ministry is not something where we have to stop what we are doing to engage in. Rather, it is something we do **while** we are living out our lives. It is not something we must always go and do. It is also something we do **as** we go. It is something we do not dread doing, but rather something we take great joy from doing.

You are definitely shaped for ministry through your Spiritual Gift(s).

Now that you know or are close to knowing your Spiritual Gift, you can begin to think about the other factors which come into play when attempting to discover your ministry.

You can also be shaped by God for ministry as He Speaks to Your Heart. The Bible defines your heart as the organ that pumps your blood, your emotional constitution or disposition (i.e. I just don't have the heart for it), and the vital force or driving impulse (i.e. that team just doesn't seem to be playing with 'heart'). You worship a God who can speak directly to your heart, out around your senses – directly to your heart. Your heart determines why you say the things you say, why you feel the way you feel, and why you act the way you do. Your heart is the real you ! God has given *you* a unique heartbeat and you can do His will for you and serve His purpose by listening to your heart and letting it motivate you for ministry. How do we do that ? How do we listen to our hearts ?

To answer that, let me ask you a question. What is your heart telling you about the way God might want to use you ? When do you find yourself saying "I must do this", or "I'm looking forward to doing this", not "I ought to do this"? In other words, with regard to your Christian service, what excites you ? What is your passion ? We hear people saying all the time, "My passion is children", "My passion is seniors", or "My passion is discipleship….witnessing….evangelism". How do you answer that question ? Or try this question, "With regard to my Christian service, I love   to …..?" God speaks to our hearts by placing these passions in us. Let me give you an example or two.

One young man I met at a week-end told me that his passion was young people. He went on to say that as a young person he had given up on the church and for almost two decades, no one spoke with him about the church or his relationship with Christ. When he rededicated his life to Christ, he told the church, "I wasted almost twenty years of my life and if I can do anything about it, I won't let that happen to the young people I encounter – I guess you could say I have a passion for young people."

Another young man told me about an incident in his life which illustrates how God sometimes speaks to our hearts. He told me that he drove past a vacant lot every day on his way to work. It was filled with trash and a few abandoned cars. He remembers thinking one day, why couldn't someone clean up that lot and give the neighborhood children a place to play? It bothered him every day. He said he even changed the way he drove to work so he wouldn't have to see it and be reminded of it. But each time he turned away from that vacant lot, he remembered why he was turning and so **that** didn't work. One day he mentioned it to a friend at lunch and asked him if he thought it was a good idea to clean it up for a playground. The friend just looked at him and said, "Well Jim, I can see it's important to you." "No, no", Jim replied "Isn't it important to **you,** too?" His friend just shrugged his shoulders and said, "Well, I guess so."

Why was this bugging him? Jim couldn't figure it out. So finally, one day he decided to act. He looked up the owner of the lot, called him, and asked if it would be ok if the lot were cleaned up and the cars hauled away. The man said it was fine with him. Jim told a few friends that the upcoming Saturday was a work day at the vacant lot and if they chose to help him, that would be great. They got a lot done that first day. One of the group who was helping knew someone who had access to heavy equipment. A week later, the abandoned cars were removed. Then something miraculous (in Jim's mind) happened. While they were finishing the cleanup one week-end, a man approached Jim and said he worked for a company that manufactured playground equipment and wondered if Jim would like for his company to donate some playground equipment. He had watched the clean up for several weeks and was impressed with what Jim and his friends were doing. Today there is a playground on that vacant lot because someone listened to their heart. Was God speaking to that young man ? I don't know of course – what do you think ?

This story comes from my own church. A very active member of my church approached a staff member one day and asked him if he had ever considered starting a ministry for the mentally challenged individuals in the area. He responded by saying he had never thought about that possibility. This woman told him that she felt God was calling her to start such a ministry and would he support her attempt at our church ? The two worked together, and what started as a very small worship service on Sunday morning eventually became the largest ministry of its kind in the state of North Carolina. This lady was frequently called upon to speak in other churches on how to start a ministry of this type, She never failed to mention that she was no one special - she just listened to her heart !

What is your heart telling you ?

CHAPTER 6

A third way God speaks to us about **what we might do as a ministry in His name is through our Skills and Abilities.** One Christian leader put it this way : "Your strengths (abilities) and talents are God's gifts to you; what you do with them are your gifts to God."

"There are different kinds of working, but the same God works all of them in all men."
I Corinthians 12:6 NIV

"I God...have given him skill, ability, and knowledge in all kinds of crafts..." *Exodus 31: 3 NIV*

Here are five myths or misconceptions about abilities :

• Myth #1 - People aren't born with skills. All skills must be learned by experience. This is simply not true. There are a number of talents which seem to be inborn, or are developed very early in infancy. When people say, "He just seems to have a natural talent for it" - it's may be true !

My sister and I both started taking piano lessons at the same time. She was three years old; I was six. We both practiced the required amount of time (she probably less than me as I recall). We continued for about three years. When I asked my mother if I could stop taking lessons, she agreed. My sister was far better than I was at that time. I know, because we played duets together and she never made a mistake ! To this day, listening to Country Gardens is difficult for me because it dredges up all those old memories of not measuring up. I went on to college graduating with a science degree and she ended up with an undergraduate double major in Composition and Organ and finally a PhD in Composition. She was the head of the Department of Music at Carnegie Melon University for a number of years, retiring just recently. Don't tell me that she wasn't born with musical talent I would never hope to equal !

• Myth #2 - The skills which must be learned, are learned primarily in the classroom. Actually some of your most basic skills were learned at home, "on the street", or somewhere else outside the classroom. Toward the end of my corporate career, among a number of courses I created and presented, was a class on Business Negotiation using material I gleaned from a number of sources. The primary source of my information however, was the experience I had acquired from my 33 years in the corporate world. You can teach negotiation principles, but nothing can come close to the impact of actually negotiating with another individual who does not necessarily possess the same ethical standards you do. That is learning, as we say, 'on the street'.

• Myth #3 - If you have certain abilities, you will be very

aware of them. Again, this is not true. You are probably using a number of talents or skills of which you are not even aware. You need some process of skill identification. Try this sometime . When you see someone you know well with what appears to you to be an extraordinary talent or skill, ask them about it and listen to the response. Many times you will hear something like, "Oh this ? That's nothing special !" Those engaged in exercising these special talents are often not even aware that it is so special.

A young mechanic I met once in a transmission shop in Northern Virginia demonstrated this point beautifully. My car had broken down and needed a rebuilt transmission. We were visiting close by so I went to the shop and asked him how it was going. He showed me my transmission laid out in pieces on the garage floor. There must have been a million pieces, nuts, bolts of every description and parts of every shape imaginable. I guess my mouth dropped. I said, "Can you get all this back together ?" I was thinking of what my dad once told me. He said, "Son, any fool can take something apart but it takes real skill to put it back together." The mechanic answered, "No problem", "I've been doing this for years." "Who taught you ?", I asked. The reply, "No one really, I just started doing it myself !"

• Myth #4 – Skills that I use at work are only usable in that environment. I couldn't use them in ministry. Hopefully by the end of this book you will see the fallacy of this idea. Business skills are readily transferable to ministry as we will demonstrate.

• Myth # 5 – Most people have only a few abilities. The truth is that many national studies have proven that the average person possesses from 500-700 skills !

What about you ? What unique abilities do you have which many others do not ? What do you find relatively easy while others say. "Not me !" Have you ever surprised yourself by finding out that you could do something which you thought you could not ? Take a look at the list which follows.

Abilities & Skills List

Crisis Mgmt.	Office Skills	Knitting
Signing for Deaf	Business Mgmt.	Compose Music
Foreign Language	Assisting Migrants	Sewing
Elder Care	Working with Phys. &	CPR
Gardening	Mentally Challenged	First Aid
Assisting the Poor	Small Gp. Leader	Life Guard
Mentoring Youth	Water Purification	Diving
Memorize Scripture	Electricity	Snorkeling
Preaching	Witnessing	Typing
Repair Appliances	Livestock	Beautician
Any Sports	Radiology	Light / Sound
Furniture Repair	Nutrition	House Cleaning
Teaching Bible	Pharmacy	Store Clerk
Farming	Eye Care	Web Site Design
Disaster Relief	Dentist	Aviation
Driving Trucks	Other Med. / Dental	Programmer
Sourdough Bread	Carpentry	Radio Tech.
Needlepoint	Construction	Sales Rep.
Woodworking	Roofing	Public Relations
Flower Arranging	Heavy Equip.	Communications
Negotiation	Brick Laying	
Mediation	Welding	
Motorcycle Riding	HVAC	
Painting / Artwork	Sheetrock	
Sculpting	Computer Present.	
Creative Writing	Weather Forecasting	
Poetry	Auto Repair	
Reporting Dance	Counseling	
Home Decorating	Antique Specialist	
Retirement Planning	Table Waiting	
Fishing	Hunting	
Public Speaking	Taxidermy	
Quilting	Sheet Metal Work	
Ceramics	Listener	
Ham Radio	Making Jewelry	
Cake Decorating	Music	
Financial Counseling	Drama / Acting	
Taking Pictures	Camping	
Cooking / Baking	Outdoor Survival	
Childcare	Tax. Prep.	
Teaching Children	House Painting	
Computer Skills	Candle Making	

How could you make a ministry out of a skill or ability you have ?

Let me give you an example or two. A young lady in Idaho who trained years ago as an RN, wrote me after a week-end and this is what she said:

"I have a strong desire to do pedicures for women whom I have learned need my help. To date, I have done the feet of women who have been in recovery from openheart surgery, breast cancer, stroke, fractured hip, or hip replacement. Three of these women were in their 70's or 80's and can't reach their feet and needed a visitor. Not all were Christians. I listen, pray silently or if they wish, touch, hug, cry, teach and mainly just show up. I love every minute of it. I get right down on the floor and work with their feet. I don't care how badly the toes, bunions, corns, are. My years as a Registered Nurse prepared me for just this ministry."

Skill of Pedicures/Nursing. Ministry to ill and recovering surgical patients.

Here's a personal example:

"When my brother-in-law suffered a heart attack several years ago, my wife and I visited him in the hospital. In the corner of the room was a very small, plastic vase with a flower or two in it and some baby's breath and a few ferns. I asked my brother-in-law, "Who brought the 'flowers' ?" He replied, "Read the note." Then I noticed a small piece of paper tied to the flowers. This is what the note said :

"These flowers were in the worship

service on Sunday. They heard the music, they heard the sermon and they heard the prayers which were lifted up for you. They are a reminder to you that many are praying that you may soon rejoin us – we miss you."

I was startled. "Who did this ?", I asked. He replied, "A lady in our church. Every week, she takes the flowers which are donated for the morning worship service, breaks them into several small vases like this one, places a note on each and spends the rest of the week delivering them to shut-ins and those of us who are ill in hospitals. Next week, she starts all over again. In this church, when you give flowers, you don't take them home with you after the service !"

Skill of Flower Arranging. Ministry to church members absent from worship services.

Here's another example :

A man in North Carolina handed me a small card after a week-end in North Carolina which detailed what a woman he knew has been doing for years. This is what it said :

"A woman thought about her experience after her husband died and how hard it was when support dwindled after 2-3 weeks. So, this is what she does. She checks the obituary in her local paper daily. She keeps a record of those who have lost their husbands. Two to three weeks later, she makes up a care package with a freshly-baked loaf of bread. She goes to the home of the newly-widowed women on her list and delivers the care basket and offers a listening ear. Often, she is invited in on the spot. She has led many people to the Lord through this unique ministry."

Skill of Bread Making. Ministry to newly widowed women.

Skill of Aviation/Piloting an aircraft. Ministry to medical patients flying them in your aircraft with your fuel, to major medical facilities for treatment when the patient cannot afford to pay commercial fares.

Skill of Bass Fishing. Ministry to other fishermen on the bass tour by conducting optional Bible Studies and prayer times before and after the day's fishing event

Whether it is hanging sheet rock, electrical work, riding a motorcycle, tax preparation, candle making, radio broadcasting, cake decorating, dental technician, beautician, first aid, house painting or any one of a thousand other skills &/or abilities, it can be made into a ministry, *if* you are willing to give it back to the Lord in service to others.

So, I ask again, what about you ? What skills do you have ? Can you make a ministry out of one of those skills ? Have you ever thought about it ?

Take another look at the list and Name 28 specialized abilities you have and think about how you could make a ministry out of one of them !

There are at least two other ways God speaks to us regarding our personal ministry arena.

The first of these is **through your Personality**. What happens when we try to serve outside our area of giftedness ? We feel uncomfortable. It usually takes extra time and effort. Finally, even with the extra effort, we frequently do less than a wonderful job.

One example comes to mind in my own life. A friend of mine told me that he had been asked to chair the Stewardship Committee at our church for the upcoming year. This involved putting together a detailed budget, presenting it to the church for input and approval, and then promoting that budget to the church as they pledged to support it. He told me this: "I'm the perfect person to do the detail work behind the scenes, about where the money goes and how much is spent here and there. But I am **not** the person to speak to the congregation about the budget and the last person to try to promote it and ask for support in pledging to it. You are the one to do that." What he proposed to me was somewhat radical. He proposed that we do it together. He would handle the detail and I would be the 'front' person as he described me. Well, that was the first time that was ever done in our church, but it worked like a charm. Both of us using our personality to do what we were perfectly suited to do and feeling no pressure to do what would have been difficult or impossible for either of us to do alone.

That's one way we can look at personality as we serve. You may be the chairperson of a church committee. However, it may be very beneficial to allow someone else in the group to lead out in a certain area or at a certain point in the committee's work, where it fits his/her personality.

God has given us this tremendous diversity in the way we think and act. The important thing is to not get caught up in believing that the way **we** think and act is always the best.

From my experience in teaching team effectiveness in the corporate world, I know that personality is a very complex subject. Now, with that in mind, I want to look at a relatively simple personality model and see how it might be useful to apply that model to how the church does its business.

First, the model – Generally speaking :

I. Extravert or Introvert ?

Extraverts tend to think **while** they are talking. Introverts, on the other hand, believe in thinking **before** they speak. Therefore, Extraverts need time to talk and Introverts need time to think. Extraverts go to a party and decide if it's a great party when and only when they have met and spoken to everyone at the party. This may take some time ! Introverts, on the other hand, can spend the entire evening on the patio speaking to only one or perhaps two people and have a great time. When it comes to meetings, Extraverts don't need an agenda. They simply believe anyone should be able to just start talking about a subject the way they do and give an opinion without a lot of pre-thinking. In other words, they think **while** they are talking. Introverts love agendas. They can study and think about the subject before being asked to give an opinion. In short, they can be prepared to speak especially if someone asks them to ! Do we need Extraverts

and Introverts ? My answer is yes ! We need both. Extraverts get the conversation going and allow time for the Introverts to think about what they are going to say. Do we need to learn how to communicate with those who are different from us ? The answer is definitely – yes !

II. 'Big Picture People' or 'Detail People'?

The Big Picture People see what's coming before the rest of us. They love to be able to see where we are going and to tell you how great it's going to be when we get there. These are the dreamers – the predictors. If you say to one of them, "Did you know that was going to happen ?" They are liable to say, "Yes, I thought about it and saw that what happened was a real possibility." "Then why didn't you tell us at the time ?" you might say. "Well", they reply, "At the time, I thought about a lot of things that might happen and that was just **one** of them." In other words, these people are good at looking through all the options and possibilities, but they themselves can't always predict what will happen – just know that they will have thought about it before hand.

The Detail People, on the other hand, are not so much interested in the future as they are in right now. They say to the Big Picture People, "I heard what you said about where we are going in the future, but what I am interested in is the first thing you want me to do tomorrow morning" ; i.e. the details. As they are fond of saying : "The Devil is in the details!" "Yes, it's going to be great in the future, but right now, things are a mess and I just want to know the steps we should take right now to get to your bright future ?" They love step by step processes and are only interested in the practical here and now. "That's the only thing that counts", they say.

Do we **need** both ? Do we need Big Picture people **and** Detail People ? Sure we do ! Big Picture People show us the way. They encourage us to continue when the present isn't so great but the future looks so terrific. But, the Detail people are the ones who supply the details. They are the ones to say, "Here are the steps we need to take right now to begin to walk towards the future you just described".

III. Head (Thinking) or Heart (Feeling) ?

The Head people believe that the only criteria for a decision is asking the question, "Is it logical and / or rational?" It doesn't mean they are insensitive to others or don't think of others. It simply means that the way others might **react** to a decision is not their first priority. (In fact, the way others might react sometimes get lost entirely !).

Conversely, Feelers tend to consider a course of action in the light of whether someone might or might not like that course of action. (What tends to get lost here is whether or not it is a **logical** or **rational** decision !). Head people tend to say, "Then, since **that's** the logical thing to do, that's what we'll do." Feelers respond, "Well, Frank (or someone else) is not going to like it !" This news is not likely to be received by the Head folks as terribly helpful ! The response might be something like, "Well, that's just tough – Frank will just have to get used to it !" Well, you get the picture.

Do we need Head **and** Feeling folks ? Of course we do ! We need the Head folks to make sure what we decide is logical and rational. We certainly need the Feeling folks because they are the ones who will know how well the decision will go down with those who will have to buy into it to make it successful.

I found this out in a real way in my corporate life. I was part of a management staff of five who met weekly and made decisions about how our small business would operate. We made manufacturing, marketing, and administrative decisions every time we met. It was only after a year or so when one of the staff called it to our attention, that many of our decisions never got acted upon. When we inquired about this with a few outspoken employees, we found out why. There were no Feelers on the staff and according to the feedback we got, no one took the time to ask how our decisions would be accepted. They were always good, logical decisions, but….without feedback from those who thought differently than we did, those very same decisions never got implemented. Needless to say, we changed the way we operated. We secured the confidential assistance of a few Feeling type employees who could be trusted to give us their view as to how a potential decision would be seen by the rest of the work group. In time, our decisions were implemented and we got credit for being really sensitive to our employees. No one ever knew that we were not the sensitive ones ! We just learned how to listen to those who were !

III.Structured, Decisive or Unstructured and Spontaneous ?

Structured People love closure and making decisions. They keep prioritized lists of projects ; start one, finish it, and then move on to the next project on the list. They even put things on the list they have *already finished* because they take such great joy from crossing off things on their list !

Ask the Unstructured People group what they think of that approach and you'll get something like, "That's sick !" "The only way to really enjoy what you are doing, is to start something and then move on to something else whenever the spirit strikes you. Don't get caught up in all that list-making junk !" If the plan's not working, this group will pitch the plan in a New York minute and start a new one !

With the Structured group, when the plan fails, they will spend a lot of time trying to analyze why it is failing and strive to make it work – they don't like giving up the plan. "So what happens if a decision turns out to be bad," you ask the Structured group. "That's easy," they say, "Just make a another decision. !" The Unstructured group puts off making the decision as long as they can to **avoid** making a mistake. There's always more information to be considered, you see.

Do we need both types ? Of course we do. We need the structured types to organize the plan and make decisions. We need the unstructured types to know when to pitch the plan when it isn't working and move on with a new plan.

So how does all this work in the church ? Let's create a fictitious group in your church called :

The First Baptist Sunday School Reorganization Committee. The pastor requested this committee be organized to make recommendations about how the Sunday School should be reorganized because he heard about a family that supposedly left the church because they couldn't find the 'right place' in Sunday School.

So, the first meeting is about to get underway with the chairman (an Extrovert) making an opening statement. It is quite lengthy and after it is over, several others (mostly Extroverts) speak up and add their input, all in support of a major reorganization. The chair realizes that some of the quieter members haven't spoken up and wants to display his sensitivity so he asks one of them, "Jim, what do you think ?" Jim, an Introvert, speaks up, "Is there an agenda for this meeting ?" Dave, an Extravert, and the committee chair, is taken aback by this and answers, "Why no, do we need one ?" "Well," Jim says somewhat cynically, "It **would** give us a chance to **think** about what we're doing here." "Why we don't need to think about it Jim, just say what's on your mind." "Well, I don't know what's on my mind," Jim responds – "I just want to think about it !"

Then, another member, a Big Picture Person, speaks up and describes how good it will be when the reorganization is completed. Others of like mind chime in. Then a frustrated Detail Person speaks up, "What I want to know from the Big Picture People is where do we start – what's the first step ?" None of the Big Picture People can say, of course, but another Detail person gives what can only be described as a brilliant analysis of each step in the process on the way to a completely reorganized Sunday School.

"That sounds great !" is the contribution of a Head / Thinking individual who has been quiet until now. Several other Head / Thinking individuals agree.

The chair asks, "Any more input?" A somewhat embarrassed Feeling Type speaks up and says, "You have just proposed moving the Senior Adults out of their corner classroom that overlooks the city park and into a windowless room on the first floor next to the heating and air conditioning unit which is so loud and needs to be replaced. The Young Couples will love their new corner room, but I don't think the Seniors will appreciate this decision. They bought those chair covers and one of their members donated that rug and then the draperies were sewn together by the class members. That comment really quieted the room down. But, the chair speaks up quickly, "Thanks for that input Shirley", "Are there any other comments?" Shirley quietly fumes. She brought up her concern and it was ignored. Well, the next time they ask for input, Shirley will most likely keep her concerns to herself or perhaps stop coming to the meetings altogether.

"So then," a Structured and Decisive member says, "Sounds like we're ready to vote?" "All those in favor of……..", the chair begins. "Wait a minute", an Unstructured /Spontaneous member speaks up. "Do we have to vote right now?" "What do you propose Barry?", the chair responds. "Well, do we have to vote on the same night we're having the discussion?" "Why, what else do you want to say about it Barry?" the chair replies? "I don't know what else I want to say – I just want to think about it some more" is the answer.

So it goes, on and on. Personality enters into the picture every time we get together in the church.

But many times, instead of celebrating the great diversity of personality **which God has given to each of us**, we, in the church, attempt to shut out those who disagree with us or with the way our minds are structured. In the beautiful words of Og Mandino,

> "Strive not to walk where your brother has walked, nor talk as your leader talks. Imitate no one ! Be yourself ! You bring value to the world. Let your wondrous personality shine through !"

"Psalms 139: 14 says, "I will praise you because I am fearfully and wondrously made." NIV

So wondrously made of course, that it is impossible for us to map any personality no matter how complex a model we may construct. But respect for another opinion or another approach besides the one **I** prefer, that is something we can all work toward.

That brings us to the last method which we will discuss about how God speaks to us to prepare and SHAPE us for ministry – **Our Life Experiences.**

What do you think about this quote from one Bob Reccord :

"God reveals His mission for you through His Word, His Spirit, the wise council of others *and His work in circumstances around You.*"

Paul said it this way,

"And we know that in all things God works together for good of those who love Him and are called according to his purpose." Romans 8:28 NIV

As a Christian, we develop through spiritual experiences, painful experiences, educational experiences, work experiences and ministry experiences; and sometimes we can find our ministry through them also.

Let's take Paul the Apostle as an example. He said this about his life :

"Now I (Apostle Paul) want you to know, brothers, that what has happened to me has really served to advance the gospel." Philippians 1: 12 NIV

It is certainly true that Paul had dramatic **spiritual experiences**. Remember the Damascus road experience where he was struck by a blinding light and when he asked, "Who are you Lord?" The answer came immediately, "I am Jesus whom you are persecuting." This experience was central to Paul's preaching after that. Or how about the dream he had which turned him and his mission efforts toward Macedonia? Then remember the scene in the jail when an earthquake shook the ground ? The prison doors flew open and his chains were loosed. Paul did not leave but stayed with the jailer and after witnessing to him and his family, all became believers in Christ. These are just a few of Paul's spiritual experiences.

It is also true that Paul had many **painful experiences**. He was beaten on many occasions. He was shipwrecked and almost perished. He had some sort of malady which he described as a thorn in the flesh. He suffered under house arrest on more than one occasion. He was bitten by a poisonous snake and survived. All of this because he was constantly preaching Christ as the way of righteousness with the Father.

His **educational experiences** also were noteworthy. When Paul's credentials were questioned, he responded quickly. He was educated at the feet of Gamaliel, an outstanding teacher of Rabbinic law. In his own words, Paul described himself as a Pharisee of the Pharisees. Paul was so schooled in the Jewish law that he was able to critique the Pharisees who prided themselves in being able to tell other Jews how to live Godly lives.

His **work experiences** as a tent maker permitted him to be essentially self-sustaining throughout his life. Those skills brought him into touch with others of like mind as he led them to Christ.

His **ministry experiences** were legendary. His journeys involving the starting and encouragement of churches all around the Mediterranean Sea, encompassing over a thousand miles all the way to Rome where interestingly enough, he arrived as a prisoner, not as an evangelist as he intended. Paul used his life experiences constantly as examples of the way God was using him to spread the gospel.

The point here is this : What about **your** Spiritual experiences ? What about **your** painful experiences ? **Your** educational experiences ? **Your** work and/or ministry experiences ? Is God patiently waiting for you to make a ministry out of one of these ?

One young lady I know decided that her divorce had been so painful that she did not want others to go through a similar experience without help. She did some research and conducted a class on Divorce Recovery through her local church. It was very well received and now, through her encouragement, additional classes are being prepared. This is one example of a painful experience turned into a potential ministry. You could probably tell many more stories similar to this one.

A pastor I met in North Carolina organized a support group for parents of children with a rare bone disease after his only son died of the disease. He told me it was agonizing for him and his wife when they were going through this that there were no resources he could find for help. So, they decided that **they would become the support** for others going through this ordeal.

There are countless other stories of individuals who, after passing through a painful time in their lives, decide to make the pathway smoother for those who come behind them, thus making a ministry out of a painful experience.

In summary : Nothing about us is an accident; not our SPIRITUAL GIFTS, nor the way God whispers to our HEARTS, not our skills and ABILITIES, nor our wondrous PERSONALITIES, or the life EXPERIENCES which come our way. All are part of the way God has SHAPED us to be on mission with Him.

We end now as we began with the five purposes of the church. Here are five questions for you to consider as a Christian and a Biblical answer for each :

1. Worship – What will be the **Center** of my life ?

"....so that Christ may dwell in your hearts through faith."

Ephesians 3: 17 NLT

2. Discipleship - What will be the **Character** of my life ?

"Don't lose a minute in building on what you've been given, complementing your basic faith with good character, spiritual understanding, alert discipline, passionate patience, reverent wonder, warm friendliness, and generous love."

2 Peter 1: 5 The Message

3. Ministry – What will be the **Contribution** of my life ?

Jesus said, "....I chose you to go and bear fruit – fruit that will last."

John 15: 16 NIV

4. Mission – What will be the **Communication** of my life ?

"Whatever happens, conduct yourself in a manner worthy of the Gospel of Christ."
Philippians 1: 27

5. Fellowship – What (Who) will be the **Community** of my life ?

".....Christ loved the church and gave Himself for it." Ephesians 5: 25

One final question :

"David ...served God's purpose in his own generation." Acts 13: 36 NIV

Will **you** serve God's purpose in **your** generation ?

REDISCOVERING THE CHRISTIAN LIFE

The questions in this booklet are designed to prompt discussion about the material in Taft's book.

The questions and the discussion that follows may be painful but are crucial for your spiritual development. Don't fall into the trap that all the questions must be answered in one session.

Also, be aware that the discussion may take another direction through the leadership of the Holy Spirit. If that is the case, be sensitive and allow that to take place and simply continue at that spot at your next session.

Always remember to stop and pray when a prayer request is requested or indicated.

Finally, don't allow any one person to dominate the discussion. Bring in the quieter members with sensitivity, but never insist on an answer.

SMALL GROUP SESSION #1

What evidence do you see that the pews of our churches today are filled with empty people ? Why is this true ? Is it at least partially untrue as well ?

Is it true that the majority of the church's members have no clear understanding of who they are and what they have been called to be or to do as the People of God ?

In your opinion, is it true that Americans appear somewhat willing to come to church, read the Bible, and even make a small offering, but most stop short of establishing new priorities or making a tangible commitment to knowing and loving the God they profess?

How does Rick Warren's 'Baseball Diamond' help you to see God's purpose in the world ? Do you believe Warren has a point in saying Christians worship their God with their lives not just on Sunday morning ? What does that mean ?

Are today's Christians deliberately committed to building lifestyles of Ministry and Evangelism, i.e. Being Good News and Telling Good News ? Why or why not ? Is it because we are not clear about what God expects from them ?

Why do so many Christians believe joining a church is the end rather than the beginning of a life-long journey ?

All believers are called, gifted, equipped and sent into the world. Have you ever heard this before ? What does it mean to you ? Jesus is sending **you personally**. Have you thought about that before ?

Small Group Session #2

What do **you** think Paul means when he says, "Make your life a life of sacrifice" in Romans 12: verses 1,2 ?

Taft makes the point that Paul tells us to live for God's purpose and not for our own purpose. Do you agree with that ?

How many Christians do you know who are living like that ?

Paul also tells us we can discover God's will for our lives if we decide to live for His purpose (sacrificing our own wills to His will) and not our own. Is this the reason so many Christians say they want to know God's will for their lives, yet they say they cannot discover it - i.e. they haven't committed to doing it ?

What distraction(s) in your life do you feel is or are responsible, at least in part, for your lack of spiritual development ?

How has cooperating with other believers helped you in your spiritual walk ?

Which one of the ten truths about Spiritual Gifts was new or most interesting to you ?

Are you surprised that less than 5% of Christians have any idea what their Spiritual Gift(s) might be ? In your opinion, why is this ?

Small Group Session #3

What do you think of Taft's definition of a Spiritual Gift?

What do you think about Taft's list of Spiritual Gifts ?

Can you name individuals who exhibit the characteristics of each of these gifts ? What do they **do** that tells you they have that specific Spiritual Gift ?

Do you agree with the differences between Spiritual Gifts and natural talents or abilities as Taft explained it ? Do you have other examples ?

Which one of the 6 cautions about Spiritual Gifts was new or most interesting to you ?

Have you ever chastised someone for not responding to a need which you clearly saw and to which you responded ? What were the circumstances ?

Do you believe the speaking gifts are more important than the non-speaking gifts ? Do you have an example to illustrate your opinion ?

How has this study changed your view of Spiritual Gifts?

Taft uses the analogy, "If the Lord returns tomorrow, will He find you using your gifts ?" How does that strike you ? What do you need to do for you to take this question seriously ?

SMALL GROUP SESSION #4

Have you ever thought about why there is so much confusion about this subject of Spiritual Gifts ? Is the confusion at least partly responsible for why there is so little teaching on this subject ?

Read 1 Corinthians 12, verses 4,5 and 6, and react to Taft's point that the confusion may be due to mixing up the gifts themselves with the ways the gifts are used and the effects the gifts have on others when they are exercised.

The Billy Graham analogy Taft uses seems to point to the fact that there are some Sunday School teachers who don't necessarily have the Spiritual Gift of Teaching. They are successful because they teach in such a way that their Spiritual Gifts are recognized by those who come. Have you experienced this ? Taft says Sunday School teachers should involve the Spiritual Gifts of others to balance class effectiveness with issues such as welcoming visitors, contacting members through the week, mission efforts, etc. because they may be neglected otherwise. Do you agree ?

Are you clear about the differences Taft gives between Spiritual Gifts and natural talents or abilities ? Do you agree? Why or why not ?

Patience is a Fruit of the Spirit. It's what appears in my life by yielding to God's Spirit, according to Scripture. Why does Taft say that praying for patience is not scripture-focused ?

Are you comfortable with Evangelist and Pastor as roles individuals are in, not Spiritual Gifts ?

SMALL GROUP SESSION #5

In another quote from Dr. Edge, he says churches have emphasized 'coming' so much (coming to church, coming to hear my pastor, coming to my Bible Study class etc.) that many of us have come to believe that coming is the goal. Do you believe that this is true ? Are there upsides to coming ?

What are the shortcomings of looking at my faith as a 'coming' event rather than fuel for 'going' ?

Was it easier for you to find your gift through a ministry that you were already doing or to find a ministry after finding your gift ? Is there value to both approaches ?

Is your Christian service joyful ? In your opinion, should it be ?

Does it surprise you that Dr. Edge suggests that for most Christians, they will find their place of service right where they already are, at work or at home during the day ? What does that mean to you ?

Have you ever thought about the fact that the God you worship can speak directly to your heart ? He can place a passion for His service in your heart if you are willing to listen. How would you go about listening to your heart ?

How do **you** answer the question, "With regard to your Christian service, what is **your** passion ?" Do you have one ? If not, why do you suppose that is ?

SMALL GROUP SESSION #6

Have you ever looked at your skills and abilities as gifts from God ? How does that change your perspective ?

Have you ever thought about making a ministry out of a skill or ability you have ? What might that be ?

What is your reaction to the examples of those who have made ministries out of their skills and abilities ?

How has your personality influenced the way you serve God ?

Is diversity appreciated in your church or is it discouraged ?

Does the leadership in your church seek out diverse opinion ?

How has God revealed His presence or His mission for you through circumstances ?

What life experiences have you had which could become a ministry; Perhaps a painful time or a time of spiritual enlightenment ?

SMALL GROUP SESSION #7

What insight do the final five questions give you as you read through them slowly ?

What **is** the **center** of your life ? – What are you focusing on ? Is it eternal things or temporal things? What draws most of your attention ? Is Kingdom business a priority for you ?

What **is** the **character** of your life ? What means the most to you ? What are you doing about the way God has gifted you ?

What will be the **contribution** of your life ? What will be the thing you leave behind ? Will others have been touched positively and spiritually by your life ? What will the **Kingdom** impact be of your life ?

What will be the **communication** of your life ? What will others remember about how you conducted yourself ? Will your spirituality be a factor in someone else's life ?

What will be the **community** of your life ? With whom do you spend most of your time ? What kinds of people do you allow to influence your thinking ? How much of a part do Kingdom people play in your life ?

Notes

2. Church Renewal Journey, North American Mission Board www.churchrenewaljourney.net

3: Discovering My SHAPE for Ministry from Saddleback Resources www.saddlebackresources.com

5. "The problem is not": Charlie Shedd quoted by Dr. Findley Edge *The Greening of the Church* Word Books Publisher, Waco TX 1971, 9

5. "…a majority of church": Dr. Findley Edge *The Greening of the Church* Word Books Publisher, Waco TX 1971, 9

5 "…the average church member's": Dr. Findley Edge *The Greening of the Church* Word Books Publisher, Waco TX 1971, 9

6. '90% of Americans": The Pew Forum on Religion & Public Life religions.pewforum.org/reports# published in the Charlotte Observer June 24, 2008 1, 14

6. "75% of Americans": The Pew Forum on Religion & Public Life religions.pewforum.org/reports# published in the Charlotte Observer June 24, 2008 1, 14

6. "Only 70% of those affiliated": The Pew Forum on Religion & Public Life religions.pewforum.org/reports# published in the Charlotte Observer June 24, 2008 1, 14

6. "Only 25% believe there is": The Pew Forum on Religion & Public Life religions.pewforum.org/reports# published in the Charlotte Observer June 24, 2008 1, 14

6. "Fewer than half of those": Eddie Hammett *Reaching People Under 40 While Keeping Those Over 60* 2007 Chalice Press 2007 12

6. "In the decade from 1990": Eddie Hammett *Reaching People Under 40 While Keeping Those Over 60* 2007 Chalice Press 2007 12

6. "At the present rate": Eddie Hammett *Reaching People Under 40 While Keeping Those Over 60* 2007 Chalice Press 2007 13

7. "Baseball Diamond analogy" : Rick Warren, Pastor Saddleback Church www.saddlebackfamily.com/class/index.html

21. "Will you live for…" Rick Warren *Daily Inspiration for the Purpose Driven Life* 2004 Zondervan 44

26. The Three Colors of Ministry by Christian Schwarz

27. James Mahoney *Journey Into Usefulness* 1976 Broadman Press 65-83

37. James Mahoney *Journey Into Usefulness* 1976 Broadman Press 94-95

38. Don & Katie Fortune *Discover Your God-Given Gifts* 1987 Chosen Books The Motivational Gifts 17

38. "And this is where…" James Mahoney *Journey Into Usefulness* 1976 Broadman Press 96

42. "Eight million adults…" Eddie Hammett *Reaching People Under 40 While Keeping Those Over 60* 2007 Chalice Press 2007 13

42. "Since 1991,…" Eddie Hammett *Reaching People Under 40 While Keeping Those Over 60* 2007 Chalice Press 2007 13

42. "It's not about you". Rick Warren *The Purpose Driven Life* 2002 Zondervan 17

42. "Author Randy Singer puts it this…" Randy Singer & Bob Reccord *Made to Count* 2004 W Publishing Group 61

48. "The Fortunes, Don and Katie, did a survey" Frequency

of Spiritual Gifts, Don & Katie Fortune *Discover Your God-Given Gifts* 1987 Chosen Books 26

63. "God reveals His mission…" Randy Singer & Bob Reccord *Made to Count* 2004 W Publishing Group 139

65 "Worship – What will be the **Center** of my life ?" Rick Warren *Daily Inspiration for the Purpose Driven Life* 2004 Zondervan 278

ABOUT THE AUTHOR

Donald Taft has been involved with church renewal for over 30 years, first as a Lay Renewal coordinator and then as a Resource Leader in the second of the week-end series called The Lay Ministry Week-end. He assembled the material in the book in the late 80's originally as a study on Spiritual Gifts. It has been modified several times in response to feedback from Pators and others. Taft continues to teach this material regularly several times each year in churches all over the U.S.

LaVergne, TN USA
10 March 2010
175484LV00004B/1/P